CONTENTS

Curiosities of the Food	**1**	"The Whistling Oyster" / for trivia buffs / a wealth of varieties / about shells / pearls, of wisdom and otherwise / the food's food — a touch of violence / and a little sex / a rash of enemies.	**p. 5**
Gardeners of the Sea	**2**	"The world's hardest, coldest work" / a distinct personality / captains upon captains / and boats upon boats / fencing the garden / sowing / reaping / and culling / a short ride on an oyster ark / the growth of shucking houses and packing plants / "the great oyster craze" / an evening in an oyster cellar / oyster houses, saloons, and parlors / the ultimate raw bar — the street stall / a song about a bivalve.	**p.12**
Serving an Oyster	**3**	"Handled with respect" / handling live oysters / grades of shell stock / the R-month myths / about shucked oysters / shuckers then and now / more than one way to shuck an oyster / to serve him well / three types of oyster plates and a word about forks.	**p.33**
An Element of Social Existence	**4**	"The palm and pleasure of the table" / Dr. Franklin gains a spot in our hearts / taste, the "private laboratory" / Appetite / a word about wine / a universal remedy / the chemistry of restoration / lusty nourishment.	**p.44**
Recipes from the Finest Oyster Houses	**5**	Oyster Stew / Sauces / Oyster Plant / Oyster Crabs / Oyster Crackers / on the Half-shell / The Oyster Museum / Virginia Seafood Council / Maryland Seafood Marketing Authority / National Oyster Cook-Off / Union Oyster House / Felix's Oyster Bar / Maye's Oyster House / Dock's Oyster House / Sansom Street Oyster House / Grand Central Oyster Bar & Restaurant / Gage & Tollner's Oyster and Chop House / The Whisting Oyster / Parks' Oyster & Clam Bar / Parks' Oyster House.	**p.50**

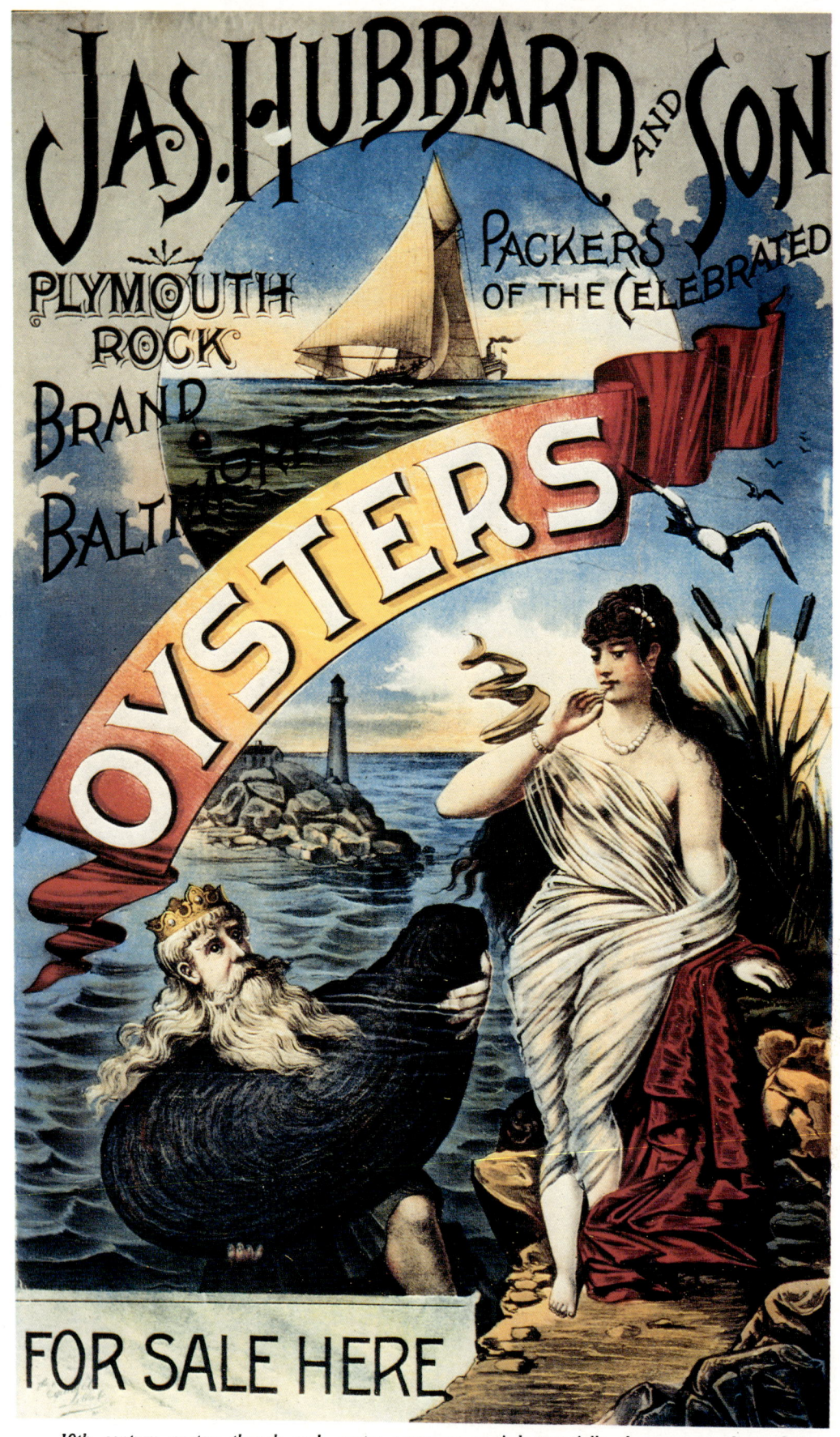

19th century poster—though each oyster company carried essentially the same product, they would attempt to out-sell each other with elaborate and romantic advertising.

A Word from the Author:

There may well be some truth in the old tale about oysters being a food for love, because I have fallen in love with oysters and you are reading the result of our affair. My family, I can confidently say, is probably the oldest continuously engaged in the seafood business in the United States, since we began to live off the sea long before the American Revolution was even thought of. Our forefathers were among the original immigrants to Tangier Island, Virginia, in the early 1700's. Fishing, oystering, clamming, and crabbing were the only industry of the island and the sole support of our family for many generations. In the twenties, my grandfather traveled through the streets of Allentown ringing his fish bell and yelling—"Here comes the fish man, get out your dish pan. Porgies at three cents a pound."

For over forty years, three generations of the Parks' Family have been selling fresh, quality seafood to residents of Pennsylvania's Lehigh Valley, and I have devoted myself to treating seafood as it deserves to be treated. A graduate of the Culinary Institute of America in Hyde Park, New York, I have worked in restaurants in West-Germany and New York. I served as senior food instructor for the Cook Training Program of the Lehigh County Area Vocational Technical School. I am currently owner and chef of Parks' Celebrated Oyster and Clam Bar in Allentown, Pennsylvania, and the co-owner of Parks' Oyster House in neighboring Bethlehem. In 1979 I was a consultant in the construction of the Mystic Seaport Museum's Victorian Oyster Saloon.

In this book, I have attempted to chronicle the history and culture of the oyster and the oyster industry, focusing primarily on the late 1800's and the romantic period known as the "Great Oyster Craze". While methods, operating procedures, and tools have changed with time, and have always varied from state to state, even from locale to locale, some general observations can be made. I have tried to capture those general observations and to remain true to the subject without becoming tedious or bogged down by scientific verbige. The text and composition are based upon years of enthusiastic research, study, and application in restaurants, fish markets, and oyster houses throughout the Eastern Shore.

These endeavors, however, were not in themselves sufficient to produce this book and I was most fortunate to be able to call upon Margit, my wife, whose patient sacrifice, courage, unique insight, and unfailing encouragement were essential to its success and publication. Jack and Jean Parks, proprietors of Parks' Seafood, provided the laboratory for my many experiments, guidance from their many years of experience in the seafood industry and their continual devotion and understanding. Mr. Frank Cagianese, my good friend and fellow collector, with enthusiasm and tireless effort was responsible for unearthing many of the illustrations in this book. Mrs. Gwen Goldman of "Gwen's Antiques" provided her friendly, faithful support over the years. She has supplied me with many unusual items of ephemera.

I would also like to thank Mr. Hillard Bloom, Tallmadge Bros. Inc.; Mr. William R. Prier, Deputy Director, Maryland Department of Economic and Community Development, Office of Seafood Marketing; and Mr. Donald Bell, Senior Sanitarian, Connecticut State Department of Health, for their expert advice and for reviewing the book for accuracy. Mr. John LaBeda, supervisor, Margolis Wines & Spirits, Inc., provided help with wine affinities. Mr. John Kochiss, author of "Oystering from New York to Boston", lent his friendly advice and kind assistance over many years. Mr. Dave Mink, proprietor, Sansom Street Oyster House, Philadelphia, is a fellow restaurateur who has always been willing to help me. Mr. John Knerr, my friend at Allentown Printing and Mr. Arthur Tarola of Lehigh Litho in Bethlehem, whose guidance, expertise and support helped me publish this book. Ms. Samantha Carol Smith's illustrations complement the authentic art, the ephemera, and the original illustrations of this book and, Dr. Thomas Gilligan's editing of the text has helped bring life to my words.

The following individuals and organizations provided invaluable research assistance: Bluepoints Co. Inc., Mr. Emil Usinger, Exec. V.P.; Shelter Island Oyster Co., Mr. John Plock; Reed and Reed Oyster Co., Mr. Reed and Mr. Neal Owens; Meredith and Meredith, Inc., Mr. J.C. Tolley; Ballard Fish and Oyster Co., Mr. C. Ballard; Mr. Chester Jones, waterman.

Gage and Tollner's (Oyster and Chop House), Mr. and Mrs. Dewey, proprietors; Grand Central Oyster Bar and Restaurant, Mr. Staub, Exec. V.P./General Mgr.; Whistling Oyster, Mr. Parella, proprietor; Garden Restaurant, Ms. Kathleen Mulhern, proprietor; Parks' Oyster House and Market, Mrs. Althea Yuracka and Mr. Mark Folger, owners; Union Oyster House, Ms. Mary Ann Milano, owner and Mr. Michael Levin, chef; Dock's Oyster House, Ms. Arlene Dougherty, proprietor; Maye's Oyster House, Mr. Dave Berosh, owner, Mr. Tony Simoni, chef; Felix's Restaurant, Mr. John Rotonti, proprietor.

Nabisco Brands, Inc., Ms. Caroline Fee, Mgr. Public Relations; Original Trenton Cracker Co., Ms. Cartlidge, V.P.; Independent Can Co., Mr. Richard Huether, Asst. Sales Mgr.; Steeltin Can Corporation, Mr. Edmund Nelson, V.P.; Carvel Hall, Division of Towle Silversmiths, Mr. Rodney Payne; R. Murphy Company, Inc., Ms. Agnes Colt, Office Mgr., Mr. Douglas Bethke, Pres.

The Old Print Shop, Kenneth M. Newman; Riba-Mobley Auctions, Mr. Brian Riba, Mr. Wm. Frost Mobley; Paper Rarities and Collectibles, Mr. and Mrs. Jeffers; Restorations by Mr. Allen Hermansader; Antique Paper Americana, Mr. Herb Page; Cape Island Antiques, Mr. Roger Crawford; Items of Americana, Mr. Thomas Gordon; Schaeffer's Books; Jean and Howard Berg; Ms. Sylvia Barrish; Mr. W.R. Taney; Mr. Joseph Freedman, a fellow collector; Mr. Paul Axler, photographer; Mr. John M. Parks, photographer; Mrs. Sandra Berry.

Maryland Historical Society, Ms. Laurie Baty, Prints and Photographs; Missouri Historical Society, Ms. Matha Clevenger, Asst. to the Curator-Pictorial History; National Museum of Natural History, Dr. Rosewater, Mr. Jack Marquardt; New Haven Historical Society, Ms. Zike, Ms. Burkepile; Oyster Museum of Chincoteague, Ms. West, Dir.; New York Historical Society, Ms. Helena Zinkham, Ms. Wendy Shadwell, Curators of Prints; South Street Seaport Museum, Mr. Roy Campbell, Design Dept.; Suffolk Marine Museum, Ms. Gertrude Welte, Mr. Roger Dunkerley, Dir.; Museum of the City of New York, Mr. Steven Miller, Asst. Curator; Seamen's Inne, Mystic, Mr. Tom Aageson, Pres.; Mystic Seaport Museum, Inc., Mr. Douglas Stein, Curator of Manuscripts, Mr. Gerald Morris, Dir. of Publications; Calvert Marine Museum, Dr. Ralph Eshelman, Dr.; Old Sardine Village Museum, Mr. and Mrs. Barney Rier; The International Historical Water Craft Society, Inc., Mr. Melbourne Smith, artist/founder; College of William and Mary, Virginia Institute of Marine Science. Mr. Michael Oesterling, Commercial Fisheries Specialist; School of Hotel Administration, Cornell University, Ms. Oaksford, Librarian; Culinary Institute of America, Special Collections, Ms. Barbara Feret, Librarian; New York Public Library Annex; Allentown Public Library, Ms. Barbara Sefranik, Librarian; Cincinatti Public Library; Dover Publications, Inc., Mr. John Grafton, Asst. to Pres.; "Food Production Management" formerly "Canning Trade", Mr. Arthur Judge II, editor/publisher; "South Jersey Magazine", Ms. Shirley Bailey, editor/publisher; "Maryland Watermen's Association", Mr. Joseph Vallient, publisher. Maryland Department of Economic and Community Development, Office of Seafood Marketing, Mr. Gordon Hallock, Dir., Ms. Vanderbeek, Fisheries Marketing Specialist; U.S. Department of Commerce, National Oceanic and Atmospheric Administration, Ms. Vicki Jones, Mr. Robert Learson, Virginia Seafood Council, Ms. Sandy Bridgeman, Admin. Asst.; Shellfish Institute of North America, Mr. Everett Tolley, Exec. Dir.; St. Mary's County Economic Development Commission, Arthur "Buck" Briscoe, Dir.

Copyright 1985 Frederick J. Parks

Additional copies may be obtained from Parks' Seafood, 435 N. 7th St., Allentown, Pa. 18102 Except where otherwise noted, all illustrations are the property of the Parks' Family Collection.
*No copies may be made of any part of this book without express permission of the author.

CURIOSITIES OF THE FOOD

In 1840, while Victoria sat solidly on the throne of England, the "Whistling Oyster" was the talk of London. On the south side of Drury Lane Theatre there was a narrow court leading out of Catherine Street and named Vinegar Yard. There, in the first half of the nineteenth century, was an oyster and refreshment room where artists and writers went to eat and gossip. It came to be known as the 'Whistling Oyster', and over the door was a hanging lamp with a big oyster painted on the sides, shown to be whistling a tune.

The shop was first opened by one Mr. Pearkes, in 1825. The Daily Telegraph reported that on a day in 1840, "the proprietor of the house in question . . . heard a strange and unusual sound proceeding from one of the tubs in which the shell-fish lay piled in layers one over the other, placidly fattening upon oatmeal and awaiting the inevitable of the remorseless knife.

"Mr. Pearkes, the landlord, listened, hardly first believing his ears. There was, however, no doubt about the matter. One of the oysters was distinctly whistling or, at any rate, producing a sort of 'sifflement' with its shell. It was not difficult to detect this phenomenal bivalve, and in a very few minutes he was triumphantly picked out from among his fellows, and put by himself in a spacious tub, with a bountiful supply of bran and meal.

"The news spread through the town,

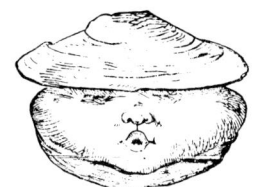

The original Whistling Oyster Signboard

Out of his depth, Harper's Bazaar, 1885

and for some days, the fortunate Mr. Pearkes found his house besieged by curious crowds . . ."

The seal is put on the story by the fact that William Makepeace Thackeray, the popular novelist and social commentator, went to see the whistling oyster and recorded that while he was in the shop, an American wag came in to see the phenomenon. After hearing the talented mollusk go through its usual performance, the American said it was nothing to an oyster he knew in Massachusetts, which "whistled Yankee Doodle right through, and followed its master about the house like a dog."[1]

Zoologically, oysters are bivalve mollusks characterized by soft bodies and hard shells. More than one hundred species of oysters live in colonies on

1) Walford, *Old and New London,* Vol. III pp. 282-284.

natural beds and banks and are found in all the seas of the temperate and torrid zones. Most oysters are found in the shallow waters of estuaries or between tidal levels in approximately 40 feet of water, though a few can be found in depths of several thousand feet.

Oysters have existed since prehistoric times when, as evidenced by fossil remains and shells found in kitchen middens of prehistoric man, they grew to enormous sizes. In the "History of British Mollusca and Their Shells", 1853, the enthusiastic oyster-eating author hovers between amazement and regret when he considers that the geologists who gazed "upon the abundantly entombed remains of the apparently well-fed and elegantly shaped oysters of the Eocene Era, 'chased pearly tears away' whilst calling to mind how all these delicate things came into the world and vanished, to so little purpose".[2]

While the hungry person is likely to regard an oyster as an oyster, not all oysters taste the same. In fact, of the many species, few are of any commercial value. And, as is true of many marine animals, the size, the shape, the flavor, and the food value of those that are even edible is severely affected by their habitat, by the foods they have eaten, and by the temperature of the water in which they have grown. Although culinary distinctions exist even among oysters in the same family, and in spite of the fact that differences can sometimes be found from one bed to another within the same locale, the epicure can still follow his taste buds on a gastronomic tour from Apalachicola to Chincoteague, then to Maurice Cove, through the Great South Bay, to New Haven and on to Belon, Maine. In legendary days, the avid oyster-eater was able to rattle off at least 400 varieties. Satirizing the excesses of first century Rome, the poet Juvenal wrote, "in our days none understood so well (as the seafood gourmet) the science of good

2) Walford, *Old and New London,* Vol. III pp. 282-284.

THE AMBITIOUS OYSTER

The oyster in his narrow bed
Complained about his lot.
"I fain wold see the world," he said,
"And leave this humble spot.
I've heard of places where the lights
Are burned 'til one A.M.,
By people out to view the sights,
I would I were with them."

He had his wish. They lifted him
Up from his briny lair.
He saw the lights — then all grew dim,
They served him up with care.
And as his shell from him they tore
These words — his last — he spoke;
"I would that I were back once more
In dear old Pocomoke."

O, Youth, with vague ambitions fired,
Despise not simple joy.
The things which most you have desired
Once gained, may most annoy.
Your fate you cannot well foresee,
Some are — the favored few —
The epicures. But some must be
The oysters in the stew.

—Anon

"Household Affairs" 1890's

eating; he could tell,
   At the first relish, if his oysters fed
   On the Ruptupian or the Lucrine bed;
   And from a crab or lobster's color name
   The country, nay the district, whence it came."

Each variety of edible oyster has, of course, developed its own following, but over the years some of the lesser names have been forgotten. Names such as Cotuits, from Cotuit Harbor, Massachusetts, or Lynnhavens, from Lynnhaven Bay, Virginia, were traditionally named after their place of origin or after the bed, bank, or rock from which they were harvested. Perhaps the most famous oyster of the 19th century was the Saddle-Rock, taken from a body of water once known as the East River which is now a part of the Long Island Sound.

The original Saddle-Rock oyster was not only very large, but it possessed a peculiar delicious flavor which gave it its reputation. The variety received its name from the rock (actually a reef) where it was first discovered, a configuration called Saddle-Rock that was twenty feet tall and fifteen feet across and resembled, when the light was right and the viewer in the proper mind-frame, an English hunting saddle. The rock was a well-known local phenomenon when in 1827, after a strong wind and a low tide, it was left bare and the retreating water revealed a bed of large oysters at its base. News of the discovery soon spread among oystermen who collected boatloads of "Saddle-Rock oysters" that soon found their way to New York City, where, on account of their excellent flavor, they commanded fancy prices even for those days. But Saddle-Rocks were not very numerous and the raking of them was so profitable that the supply became exhausted before the oystermen did, and the last of the breed slid down the throat of an unheralded New Yorker sometime in the 1830's.

The Blue Point is another well known oyster which has earned a great reputation both in the restaurant and on the market. Once known as the "Knickerbocker among oysters", Blue Points originally came from Long Island's Great South Bay, in the area off the town of Blue Point, near Patchogue.[3] The small, roundish variety found there was considered the half-shell oyster *par excellence* because of the shape, flavor, and

3) "Popular Science Monthly," Nov. 1874, Vol. VI, p. 6.

whiteness of its meat. As time went on though, any small, well-formed oyster from any part of the bay took on the magic appellation of Blue Points, and today, even though the original Blue Points are scarce, oysters with the characteristics of the Blues can be eaten at raw bars around the world.

Other oysters of note have included the Lynnhavens (favorites of Diamond Jim Brady), the Cotuits from Cotuit Harbor, Massachusetts, the Absecan Salts, the Chincoteagues (considered by many epicures as the supreme aristocrats), the Port Norris and Perth Amboys, the Belons, the Wellfleets, the Malpeques, the Narragansetts, the New Havens, the Assateagues, the Rockways, the Raritan Bays, the Roanokes, the Maurice Coves (named after the Prince Maurice which was sunk by Indians in that area), the Tangier Sounds, the Apalachicolas, the Barataria Bays, and the Shrewsburys (which were once known as the emperors of bivalves) and, the West Coast Olympia's.

Oddly enough, among the many market varieties of oysters are some that are not oysters at all. In poultry, and in veal-calves, a bit of meat closely resembles the oyster and is sometimes plucked from where it sits, oyster-like in the hollow of the bone, to be sold to unsuspecting inlanders on a fisherman's platter. And the root of a European plant called salsify, and known as the oyster plant, has a delicate oyster-like flavor when properly prepared. But no matter how adventurous the inland epicure might be, he should avoid the peculiar strain known as the *mountain oyster,* which (when choked with cocktail sauce) is considered almost molluscian but is in reality the liberated testicle of an unfortunate sheep.

Happily, sheep have no shells, and since real oysters do, the moderately sharp observer should recognize the queen of mollusks from its pauper pretenders with little trouble. If the oyster is taken in hand, it will become

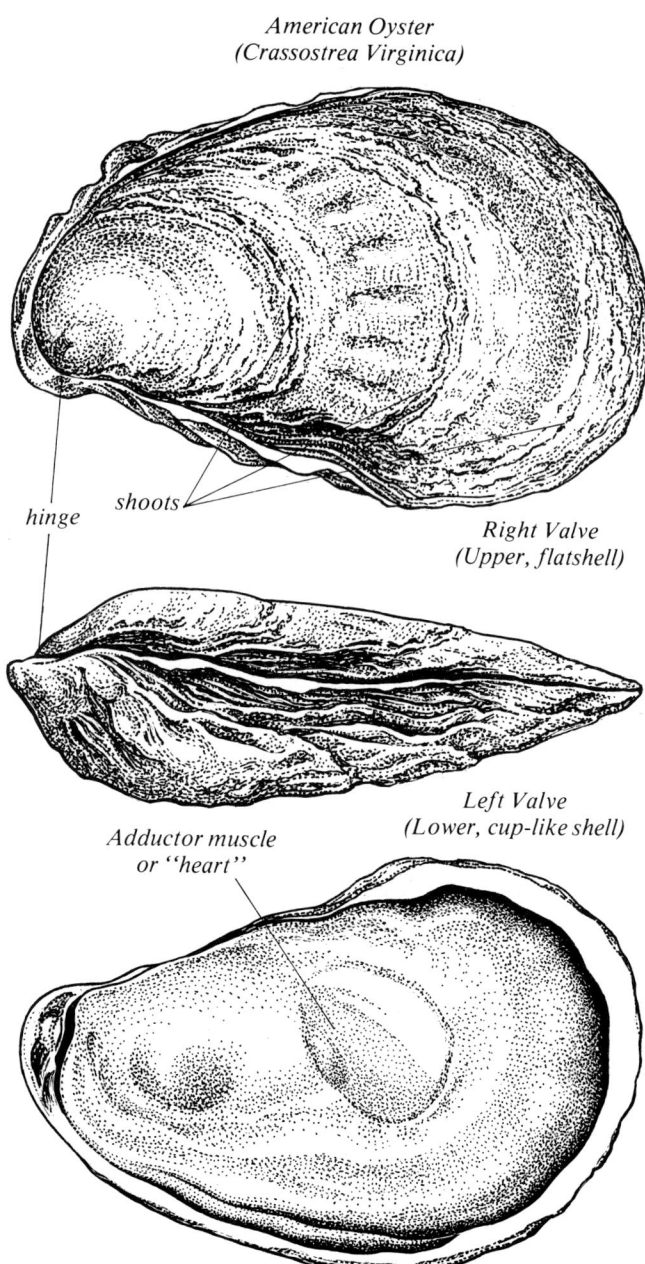

American Oyster (Crassostrea Virginica)

hinge

shoots

Right Valve (Upper, flatshell)

Left Valve (Lower, cup-like shell)

Adductor muscle or "heart"

apparent that one shell (or valve . . . Remember that the oyster, as a bi-valve, has two of them) is deeper and heavier than the other, and that it forms a sort of cup for the body. This is the bottom or lower valve, and when lying undisturbed on the ocean floor it is the underside. The upper valve is flat and covers the meat like a roof. The two valves are united by a hinge, at the narrow end, which can be tightly closed by a strong muscle. The outside of the shell is rough and irregular but the inside is polished smooth. The shell composes about 4/5ths of the oyster's entire weight and is its only means of protecting its soft body against a horde of enemies.

Oyster shells, by the way, have been used for centuries for various purposes. They have served as "metal" for roads and footpaths; as "filling" for wharfs, low lands, fortifications, and railway embankments; as cultch for new oyster beds; as ballast for vessels; as raw material for lime; as manure for exhausted fields; and as a component in mixed fertilizers. In olden times, most of the emptied shells, according to Ernest Ingersoll, "were converted into lime. There was a time when no other lime was used by the early colonists, and the mills and kilns of the New England shore towns ground nothing but oyster shells".[4]

The oyster's shell can reveal a great deal about the animal it grew to protect. "If the shell of an adult oyster be examined, it will appear to be a series of shells, lying or lapping upon each other like tiles. The upper layer is always the smaller, and the lowermost one is always the larger. The oystermen call these laps 'shoots' and each one represents a season's growth. Each shoot shows the precise size of the oyster at a given year of its life, while the sum of the entire series gives the exact number of the years the creature has lived. Nature often runs in parallel lines: the botanist counts the season-rings in the bole of a tree, the jockey tells the age of a horse by its teeth, the drover sets down the age of cattle by the rings on the horns, and the oysterman comes to a judgment by the number of shoots on the bivalve's shell. But all these specialists alike err when giving judgment upon an individual that has reached extreme old age."[5]

Lying within the shell is the body of the oyster. A thin sheet of flesh, called the

4) *The Fisheries and Fishery Industries of the United States*, Washington, Government Printing Office, Part XX-1; *The Oyster Industry* by Ernest Ingersoll, 1887, p. 563.

5) "Popular Science Monthly," Nov. 1874, p. 16.

mantle, enfolds the gelatinous mass and provides a cushioning pad for the organs. The mantle is also the shell-producing organ of the oyster and generates a substance called *nacre* which is also responsible for the formation of pearls.

When a foreign body becomes lodged within the oyster shell, the oyster begins to build a layer of nacerous material about it in onion-like, concentric layers and a pearl is born. Pearls come in many different hues and shapes but the most valuable are the large, perfectly round and flawless so-called black pearls. And certain tropical species of oysters produce pearls of irridescent lustre which are also commercially valuable, though rarely is a pearl of any importance found in oysters from North American waters, where the best an oyster seems able to do is produce a pearl that is dull and misshapen, and that resembles a bit of used chewing gum.

Since ancient times, natural pearls have been prized as objects of great worth and those of 100 pearl grains or more (25 carats) are, by their rarity, classified as treasure. In "Britannia's Pastorals", Browne gives a pleasing and poetical picture of the origin of the pearl which should increase our admiration of the jewel—

"The fair Nereides
They came on shore and slily as they fell
Convai'd each tear into an oyster-shell."

Though few mortals, perhaps, resemble the daughters of Nereus, the fiction that tears have crystallized into pearls creates an appreciation beyond price.

The oyster's shell is opened and closed by the adductor muscle and is held closed by a separate catch muscle. It is the adductor muscle, sometimes erroneously called the *eye* or the *heart,* which is severed by the knife when the shell is opened.

The strength of this muscle is considerable and several noted incidents attest to its power. In the "History of Cornwall", Carew wrote about an oyster that became a mousetrap. Apparently a dish of oysters was lying in the cellar of a local restaurant when one of the oysters opened its shell and was instantly pounced on by three mice, only to be as quickly crushed by the valves. The oyster, with the three mice dangling from its shell, was long exhibited there as a curiosity.

The edges of the oyster are fringed with rows of tiny cilia, or gills, which are soft, fleshy hairs of extreme delicacy. This fringe serves as the oyster's organ of touch. Oysters are sensitive to a number of things, including the salinity, the temperature, and the depth of the water around them, the density of the mud on which they sometimes rest, the type of ocean bottom beneath them, the currents that move past their beds, and the amount of food those currents carry. Though the sense of touch is distributed over the entire surface of the oyster's body, it is particularly acute along this hairy fringe. The fringe, which the English call the *beard,* protrudes just a little bit out of the shell, and the almost countless cilia move rapidly in the water, making, as it were, two parallel vibrating curves, which cause an aquatic vacuum inside the shell into which the water flows like a whirlpool. This stream of water brings with it diatoms, phytoplankton, and other microscopic particles of marine life which constitutes the oyster's food.

Oysters eat day and night, and the gills siphon an average of 20 to 50 gallons of water per day in order to provide the animal with enough to eat. Oysters seem to grow faster in warm waters, perhaps because of the abundance of food, and a southern oyster reaches marketable size in about two years, while Chesapeakes take three years, Long Islands four or five, and Cape Cods about six years to reach the same size. Researchers have tried feeding cornmeal to oysters in order to fatten them or to hold them for long periods of time, but this procedure has proven wasteful since the value of the

AN OYSTER BAR COMMUNITY
(1) mud crabs, (2) blue mussels, (3) puppy drum, (4) knobbed whelk, (5) starfish, (6) oyster drill, (7) gulls, (8) goby, (9) striped blenny, (10) sand shrimp, (11) blue crab, (12) oysters, (13) oyster spat.

cornmeal necessary to fatten an oyster is greater than the value of the oyster produced. Oysters are generally of marketable size when they reach three inches in length, and law requires that smaller ones be put back into the water.

Oddly enough, the oyster is bisexual. Adult oysters function as separate sexes, though changes from male to female and vice versa often occur. As soon as the water temperature is sufficiently high, oysters prepare for reproduction. The release of the male oyster's sperm and the female's ova is known as spawning. By the first spawning season, the gonads have developed in such a way that within a given group of oysters the numbers of individuals of each sex is almost equal.

Oysters are highly prolific and millions of young (or spat, as they are called) are released. The young are free swimming larvae, but change radically in form through a process called metamorphosis, then 'set' or affix themselves for life to such hard objects as rocks, reefs, or empty shells.

Congregations of oysters, or colonies, crowd one another side by side until only

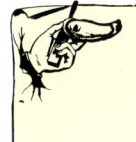

> "Oysters are terrific bivalves,
>   They have young ones by the score.
> How they diddle is a riddle,
>   They just keep on having more."

the strongest survive. Each generation is then capped and overborne by the settlement of ensuing ones, and the great masses in shallow, inshore waters are then called grounds, bars, banks, reefs, or rocks.

Left undisturbed, oysters would undoubtedly fill the seas, but their numbers are brutally assaulted by the constant depredations of disease, parasites, predators, and pollution. A disease known as MSX is particularly devastating and can cause up to 85% mortality among planted oysters. Crabs, worms, boring sponges, oyster drills, rays, drumfish and 'Five-fingers', or starfish, prey upon the mollusk in large concentrations.

And if these enemies were not enough, the unfortunate oyster also tastes good, and man, with his unsatiable appetite, is unrelenting in his efforts to harvest the delicious bivalve.

THE WALRUS AND THE CARPENTER
by Lewis Carroll

The sun was shining on the sea,
  Shining with all his might:
He did his very best to make
  The billows smooth and bright—
And this was odd, because it was
  The middle of the night.

The moon was shining sulkily,
  Because she thought the sun
Had got no business to be there
  After the day was done—
"It's very rude of him," she said,
  "To come and spoil the fun!"

The sea was wet as wet could be,
  The sands were dry as dry.
You could not see a cloud, because
  No cloud was in the sky:
No birds were flying overhead—
  There were no birds to fly.

The Walrus and the Carpenter
  Were walking close at hand:
They went like anything to see
  Such quantities of sand:
"If this were only cleared away,"
  They said, "It would be grand!"

"If seven maids with seven mops
  Swept it for half a year,
Do you suppose," the Walrus said,
  "That they could get it clear?"
"I doubt it," said the Carpenter,
  And shed a bitter tear.

"O Oysters, come and walk with us!"
  The Walrus did beseech.
"A pleasant walk, a pleasant talk,
  Along the briny beach:
We cannot do with more than four,
  To give a hand to each."

The eldest Oyster looked at him,
  But never a word he said:
The eldest Oyster winked his eye,
  And shook his heavy head—
Meaning to say he did not choose
  To leave the oyster-bed.

But four young Oysters hurried up,
  All eager for the treat:
Their coats were brushed, their faces washed,
  Their shoes were clean and neat,
And this was odd, because you know,
  They hadn't any feet.

Four other Oysters followed them,
  And yet another four;
And thick and fast they came at last,
  And more, and more, and more—
All hopping through the frothy waves,
  And scrambling to the shore.

The Walrus and the Carpenter
  Walked on a mile or so,
And then they rested on a rock
  Conveniently low:
And all the little Oysters stood
  And waited in a row.

"The time has come," the Walrus said,
  "To talk of many things:
Of shoes—and ships—and sealing wax—
  Of cabbages—and kings—
And why the sea is boiling hot—
  And whether pigs have wings."

"But wait a bit," the Oysters cried,
  "Before we have our chat;
For some of us are out of breath,
  And all of us are fat!"
"No hurry!" said the Carpenter.
  They thanked him much for that.

"A loaf of bread," the Walrus said,
  "Is what we chiefly need:
Pepper and vinegar besides
  Are very good indeed—
Now, if you're ready, Oysters dear,
  We can begin to feed."

"But not on us!" the Oysters cried,
  Turning a little blue.
"After such kindness, that would be
  A dismal thing to do!"
"The night is fine," the Walrus said
  "Do you admire the view?"

"It was so kind of you to come!
  And you are very nice!"
The Carpenter said nothing but
  "Cut us another slice.
I wish you were not quite so deaf—
  I've had to ask you twice!"

"It seems a shame," the Walrus said
  "To play them such a trick.
After we've brought them out so far,
  And made them trot so quick!"
The Carpenter said nothing but
  "The butter's spread too thick!"

"I weep for you," the Walrus said:
  "I deeply sympathize."
With sobs and tears he sorted out
  Those of the largest size,
Holding his pocket-handkerchief
  Before his streaming eyes.
"O Oysters," said the Carpenter,
  "You've had a pleasant run!
Shall we be trotting home again?"
  But answer came there none—
And this was scracely odd, because
  They'd eaten every one.

Favorite bed for small boats—gathering and dressing oysters under difficulties.
Frank Leslie's illustrated newspaper, 1879

GARDENERS OF THE SEA

When sitting and dining in the comfort of a restaurant, or in the familiar and convenient surroundings of our homes, it is difficult for most of us to imagine or appreciate the labor and hardships of the men, farmers and oystermen alike, who have harvested the food we are eating. Indeed, both farming the land and farming the oceans demand long hours of hard, physical work and constant exposure to the elements. The work of the farmers and of the oystermen is similar in detail, and the terms used by the oystermen so nearly resemble those of the farmer, that the oyster cultivator may well be called the "gardener of the sea". His oysters grow on the 'ground' which he has 'staked out' to enable him to distinguish his 'bed' from that of his neighbors, and the 'planting of seed', 'transplanting', and 'harvesting' are all terms which the oysterman applies to his 'crop'.

Oystering is the industry and culture that surrounds the marketing of oysters and has been referred to as the "world's hardest, coldest work," with some cause. The primary season for oystering is from September to March, the coldest part of the year, and as can be expected, the life led by the oystermen is of the roughest kind. Up before the rise of the sun and returning late in the afternoon, he works hour after hour in the bitter cold and icy spray of the winter wind. Hauling oysters aboard and culling are back-breaking, monotonous chores which are repeated

Opening of the Oyster Season (by Dan Beard, Harper's Weekly *1882)*
1. Dredging through the ice. 2. Oyster shell covered with young. 3. Dredging from a boat. 4. Drumfish. 5. Opening oysters for export. 6. Oyster knives. 7. Starfish. 8. Dredge. 9. Young oysters. 10. Oyster sloops at foot of West Tenth Street.

thousands of times during the harvesting season and make precious little money for all the oysterman's troubles. In the off season, as a result, many oystermen are forced to pursue other occupations in order to live. Many fish, crab, clam, catch turtles, or shoot ducks, and they literally scoop, tong, seine, dredge and drag their living from the oceans or bays. Appropriately, they are not called oystermen at all in the Chesapeake region, but "watermen". The life is not easy and it is not financially rewarding; and yet, during the height of the great 'oyster craze' in the 1800's, some 53,000 persons and 12,000 boats were engaged in the oyster business.[1] Among those people were to be found the oystermen themselves, the shuckers and canners in the large oyster houses, the scow gangs and the persons involved in transportation, the merchants, the cooks, and those in such related businesses as boat building. Hardship tends to make people look more distinctive and in an industry as large and as hard as oystering, fascinating people were bound to emerge. According to an early issue of Cosmopolitan Magazine the nineteenth century oysterman was an interesting sight. "(He is) a study in colortones in his yellow oilskin pants, his tarpaulin hat and his English jumper as he climbed into his boat and took up the oars in preparation to rowing out over the bay. His hat, which is better known as a 'sou'wester', is made of oiled canvas. His great top boots are of rubber, and his coat like his trousers, is of yellow oilskin. He is so thickly clad in undergarments and footgear as to be almost waterproof and, in fact, it takes a smart drenching to penetrate his armor."[2]

Oystermen as a class were generally poor, residing near the water and living mostly in small houses with an acre or so of land attached to the premises, and according to most accounts were respectable, moral and honorable men equal to

WHY WORRY?
I am an old man, and have had many troubles, but most of 'em never happened.

"any body of men similarly situated."[3] Nevertheless, and this may be true of any large body of men, many of them aquired the reputation of being unscrupulous, reckless, improvident, and depraved. This poor reputation probably has something to do with the fact that the disagreeable nature of the work left many boats undermanned and, as a consequence, crews were gathered as one observer put it, "from jails, penitentiaries, workhouses, and the lowest and vilest dens of the city." The crewmen were principally whites, many of whom were foreigners (with almost every European country represented), unable to speak more than a few words of English. When a crew, which usually consisted of about eight men, was necessary, the vessel owner or captain applied to a ship-

1) Ernest Ingersoll, *The Oyster Industry,* 1887, pp. 564-565.
2) "The Cosmopolitan", Vol. II, 1891, p. 720.
3) Ernest Ingersoll, *The Oyster Industry,* 1887.

ping agent, who then gathered these men wherever they could be found, drunk or sober. As one large boat owner expressed, "We don't care where he gets them, whether they are drunk or sober, clothed or naked, just so they can be made to work at turning a windlass."[4] And that same observer noted the difference between the two types of men that farmed the ocean, although he seems to have been too greatly influenced by the rowdy minority. The men, he says, "take their little pay and soon spend it in debauchery amid the lowest groggeries and dens of infamy to be found in certain portions of Baltimore. It is a gratifying fact though, that even amid such surroundings as these, there are some few respectable and honorable men."[5]

But the ranks of the oystermen have thinned considerably since the days of the great oyster craze, and the bulk of the unscrupulous, improvident men have either abandoned the industry for more lucrative and easy callings or have been 'culled-out' by the more respectable members of the community. With few exceptions, most oystermen today have followed in the footsteps of their fathers. Most are American born, and quite a few can trace their lineage to the Revolutionary War days. They are hardy, honest, resourceful, stubborn, and God-fearing men whose experience with their calling is of long standing.

An amusing aside in the story of the oystermen arises from the fact that in the old days, a visitor to an oystering community would likely find that the population was largely composed of men called captain. As Cosmopolitan reported in 1891, "whoever has owned and used a boat at no matter remote a period is always a captain". If you will venture out on the bay some morning you will find numerous vessels belonging to the fleet of oysterboats, and the master of a sloop never fails to salute the masters of the others whenever the boats are within hearing distance with a hearty 'Good

"The Creek" at Keyport, N.J. with oyster-boats, skiffs, and scows, 1888.

4) Ernest Ingersoll, *The Oyster Industry*, 1887, pp. 549-550.

5) Ernest Ingersoll, *The Oyster Industry*, 1887, p. 550.

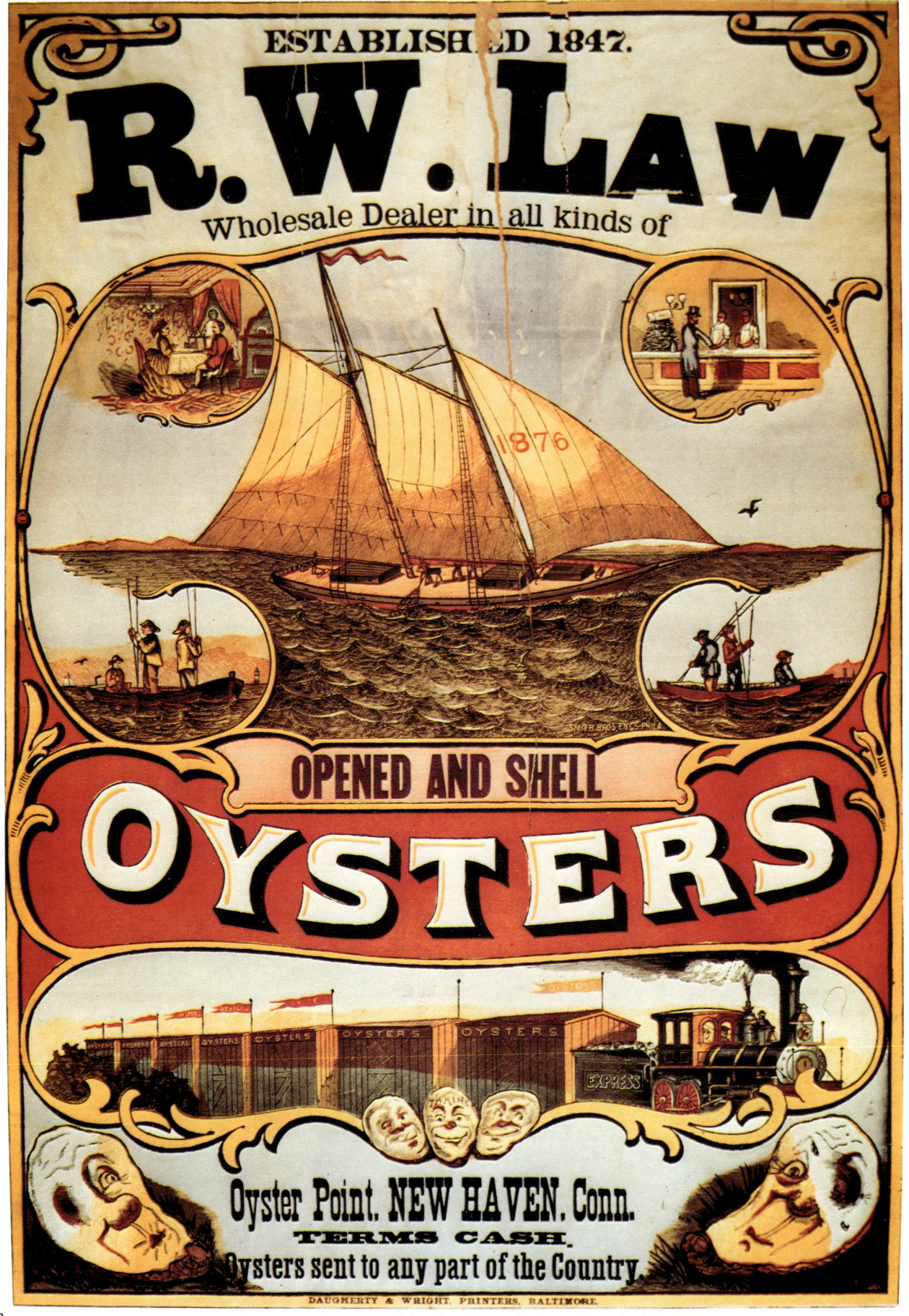

original poster Courtesy of the New Haven Colony Historical Society

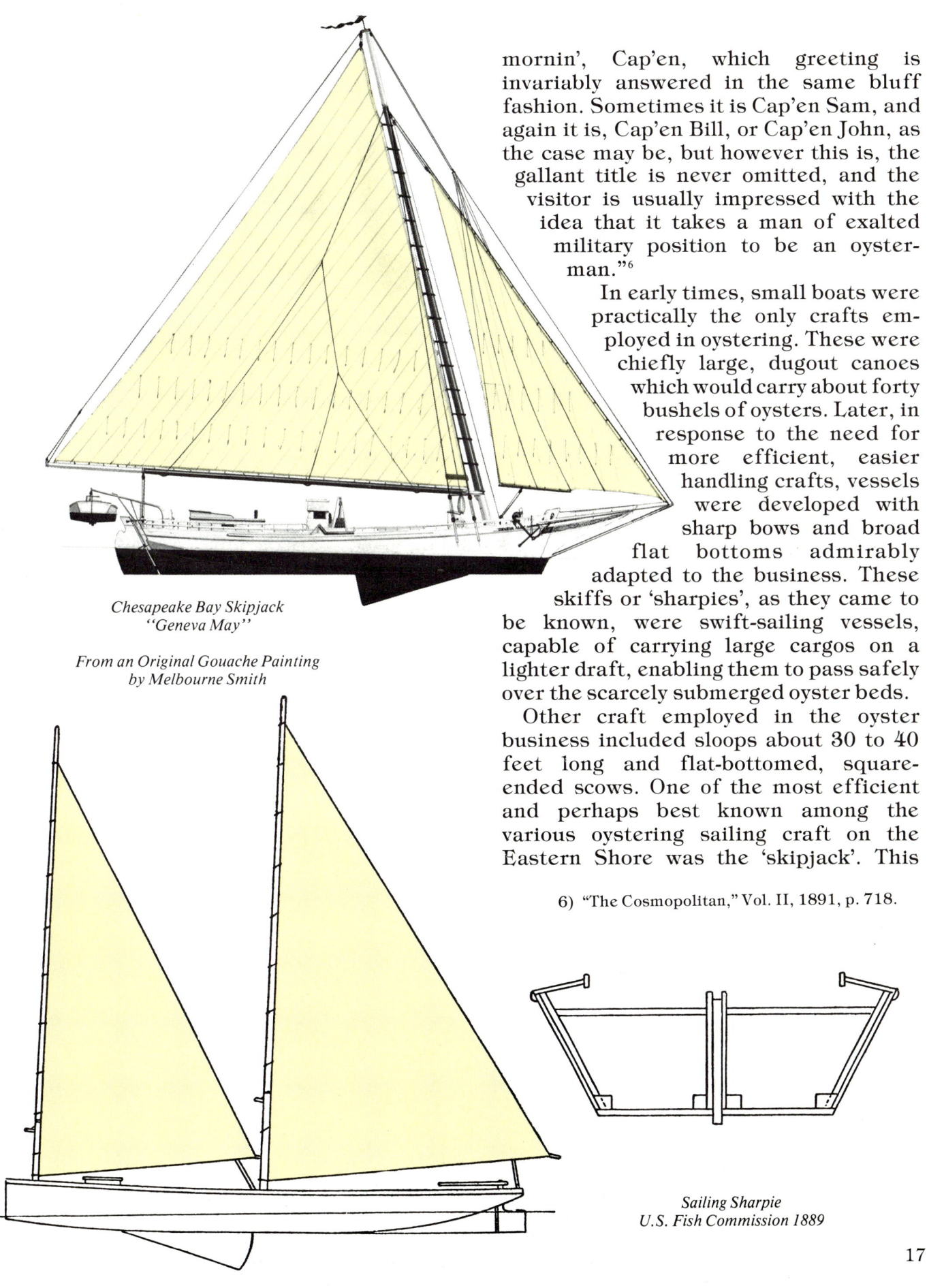

*Chesapeake Bay Skipjack
"Geneva May"*

*From an Original Gouache Painting
by Melbourne Smith*

*Sailing Sharpie
U.S. Fish Commission 1889*

mornin', Cap'en, which greeting is invariably answered in the same bluff fashion. Sometimes it is Cap'en Sam, and again it is, Cap'en Bill, or Cap'en John, as the case may be, but however this is, the gallant title is never omitted, and the visitor is usually impressed with the idea that it takes a man of exalted military position to be an oysterman."[6]

In early times, small boats were practically the only crafts employed in oystering. These were chiefly large, dugout canoes which would carry about forty bushels of oysters. Later, in response to the need for more efficient, easier handling crafts, vessels were developed with sharp bows and broad flat bottoms admirably adapted to the business. These skiffs or 'sharpies', as they came to be known, were swift-sailing vessels, capable of carrying large cargos on a lighter draft, enabling them to pass safely over the scarcely submerged oyster beds.

Other craft employed in the oyster business included sloops about 30 to 40 feet long and flat-bottomed, square-ended scows. One of the most efficient and perhaps best known among the various oystering sailing craft on the Eastern Shore was the 'skipjack'. This

6) "The Cosmopolitan," Vol. II, 1891, p. 718.

Emptying the dredgers on board the steamer "William H. Lockwood." 1879

Oyster-dredging steamer at work in Long Island Sound. U.S. Fish Commission, 1888

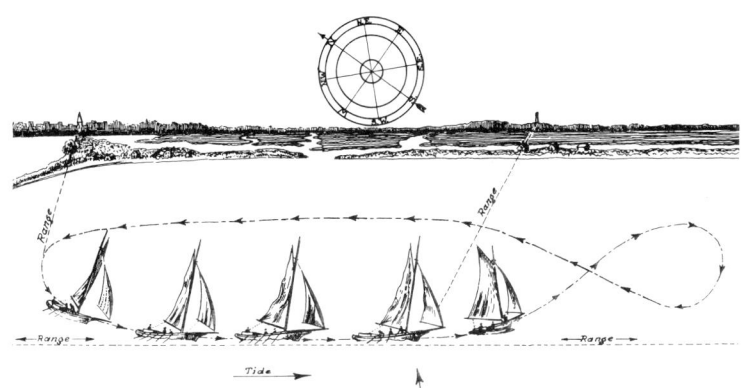

*"Oystering under Sail"
Drawing by
John Leavitt
Courtesy of
Mystic Seaport Museum*

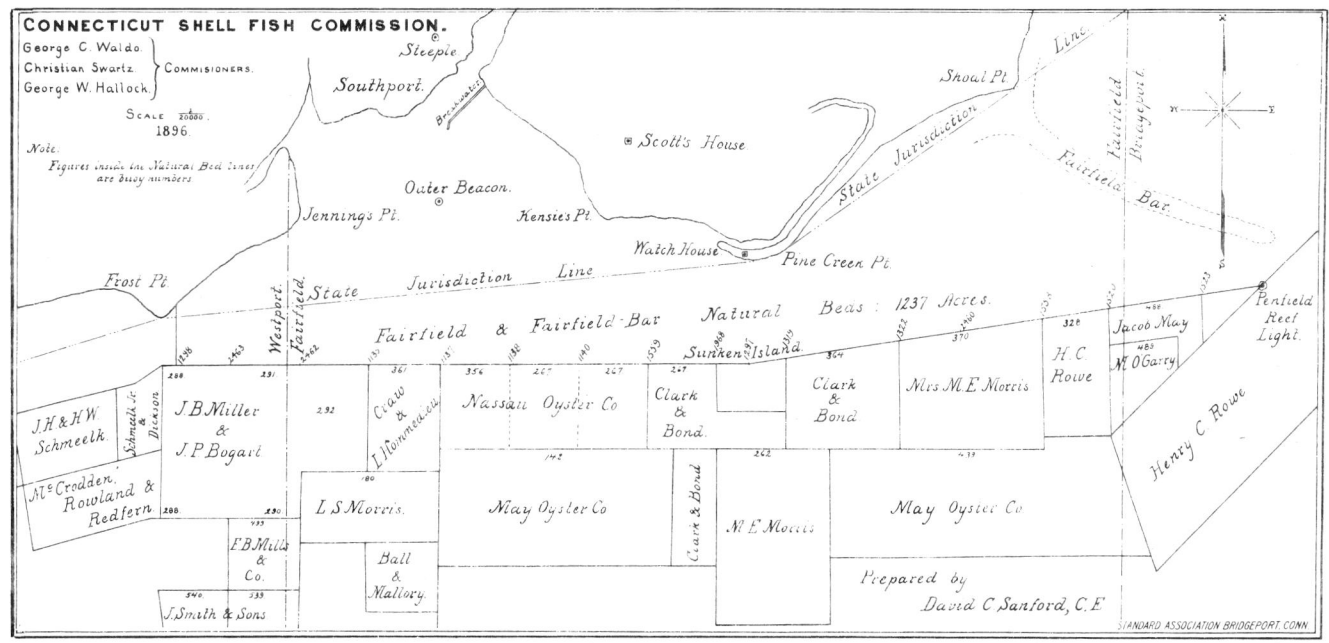

Long Island Sound Oyster Grounds, 1896. Courtesy John M. Kochiss

relatively small, easily constructed craft was developed in the late 1800's and achieved immediate success. Thousands of these sailing craft worked in the waters and filled the horizon with their billowing sails prior to the advent of the steam driven dredge boats. Today, only a handful of these sailing craft remain, but some states still reserve certain sections of the ocean or specific blocks of time in which only sailing vessels can be used to harvest oysters, thus preserving this colorful heritage of our past.

With the advent of steam-driven craft, however, many of the former sailing craft were converted into the more efficient oyster dredges. Employing large machine-hoisted dredges or suction dredges which operate on the same principle as the vacuum cleaner, modern oyster dredges are able to harvest more oysters in considerably less time. Simple economics thus forces the demise of the more toilsome and less productive sailing vessels.

Since oysters are harvested from the open, unmarked waters of the ocean, bays and estuaries, a question is often asked about how the oysterman is able to distinguish his 'bed' of oysters from that of his neighbors, but the process is relatively simple. The government, state or local, acting through oyster commissioners or other authorities, designates specific areas or grounds open to oystering. Individuals or groups apply for permits or franchises to harvest the grounds, and once approved, the oysterman then marks off his grounds with stakes—usually young scrub oaks, twenty or more feet in length and denuded of all branches

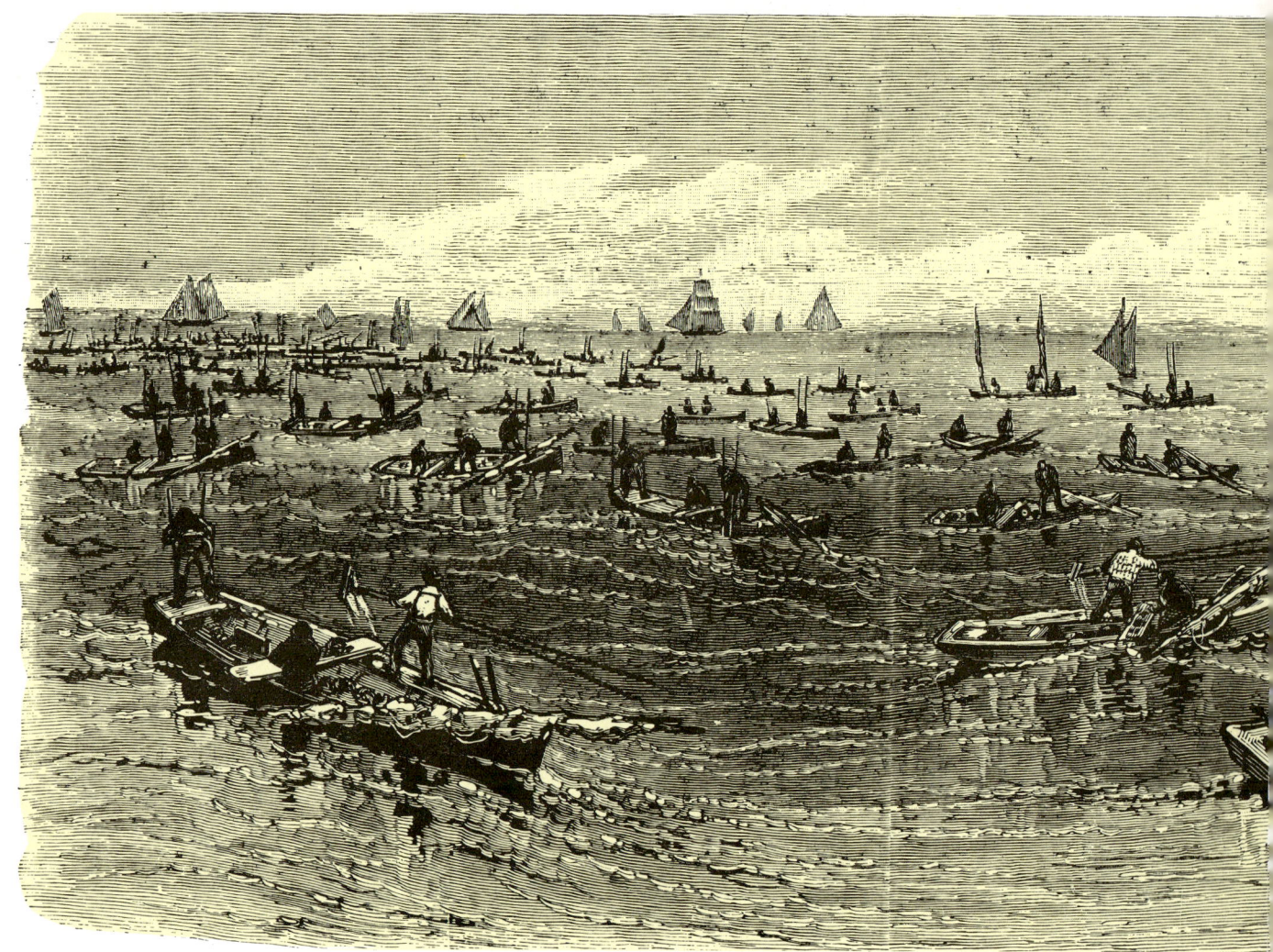

Raking for oysters off Tally's

except those at the upper end. Corner stakes are placed at the edges of the grounds and line stakes at intervals in between, and all are driven deep into the sandy bed. These stakes have their counterparts on shore which are usually prominent objects such as a light house, a sand mound, the mouth of a stream, or sometimes a house or weather fagged tree and are known as the range.

The oysterman's 'garden' is thus enclosed by a 'fence' which is easily recognized and firmly fixed in his mind, even though the grounds may be located many feet under the water. Winds and storms however, often make repairs necessary and 'staking out' is an on-going process.

While staking out is satisfactory for the individual oysterman, not all problems have traditionally been solved by this procedure. In 1889, Harper's Weekly reported that most oystermen have no respect for the law, for they look upon the oyster as a blessing of Nature not amenable to the statutes of a mere Legislature. Disputes over ownership of oyster grounds led often to a practice referred to as oyster pirating. In the 1890's, the situation became particularly inflamatory between natives of Maryland and Virginia, each group claiming undisputed ownership of the oyster grounds in the area of the Chesapeake shared by their common borders. The resultant "territorial invasion" precipitated the "Pocomoke Oyster War". Each side supported their rights by force, and fleets of oyster boats literally fought it out in the

Reef, Chesapeake Bay, 1879.

open waters of the Chesapeake. At the time, one reporter wrote, "I believe that, with the possible exception of similar incidents attending the disputed seal-fisheries in the Bering Sea, this is the only occasion since the close of the Civil War upon which canon has been fired, with hostile intent, in territory belonging to the United States."[7]

Oysters are harvested either wild from natural beds or, as is more often the case today, from cultivated grounds. Cultivation usually implies that the oyster spat is caught on shells which have been planted for that purpose and then the oysters are cared for until they reach a marketable size. Wild oysters are rough and irregular, while cultivated oysters assume a more uniform shape and produce more standard meat.

The first process in oyster cultivation is the spreading or planting of shells or other hard material called "cultch" in the water on "setting ground" to permit an adequate material upon which the oyster "spat" or "seed" can attach itself and "set". The newly settled or metamorphosed oyster adhere to the cultch and begin growing.

As these seed oysters begin growing, they may be removed to a "holding ground." This process is called planting and is done to insure better growth and to free the "setting ground" for the following year's shells. In 3 to 5 years, the oysters mature and an acre of ground generally yields about 500 marketable bushels of

7) "Lippincotts Magazine," May, 1895, p. 706.

them. In early spring, the mature oysters are often transplanted to "fattening grounds" in waters closer inshore for a few months prior to shipment to market to increase their size and flavor. Very seldom are oysters grown on the same ground from seed to market size, primarily because the needs of a two-year-old oyster and a two-month-old oyster vary considerably. These practices of moving oysters to different grounds are every bit as necessary as fertilization is to the farmer to insure the success of his crop.

In order to harvest his crop, the oysterman, like the farmer, rises early in the morning. He must do his work at ebb tide and frequently he leaves at one or two o'clock in the morning. Flood tide drives him home again late in the afternoon. In some States, however, it is now illegal, because of the safety risks involved, to work before sunrise or after sunset.

Oysters are harvested by various means. Hand tools such as rakes, tongs, nippers, and grabs are still used, though they are not as efficient as the dredge or the suction dredge. The rake, or bull-rake, was one of the first implements used for obtaining oysters from their beds. The rake has a long handle for gathering the mollusk in moderately deep water, and the tines of the basket are curved in a convex semicircle to allow the oysterman to scoop up his catch. But perhaps the most widely used and popular hand tool still in use is the hand tong. Tongs are basically a pair of opposing rake-like baskets with curved teeth. These are in turn attached to poles (up to twenty feet in length) and fastened like a pair of scissors. Patent tongs, used primarily in the Chesapeake, are a modification suited to waters too deep for hand tongs. Nippers and grabbers are similar in construction but generally hold fewer oysters and are not as extensively used.

The oyster dredge consists of a metal frame with a scraping edge and a basket

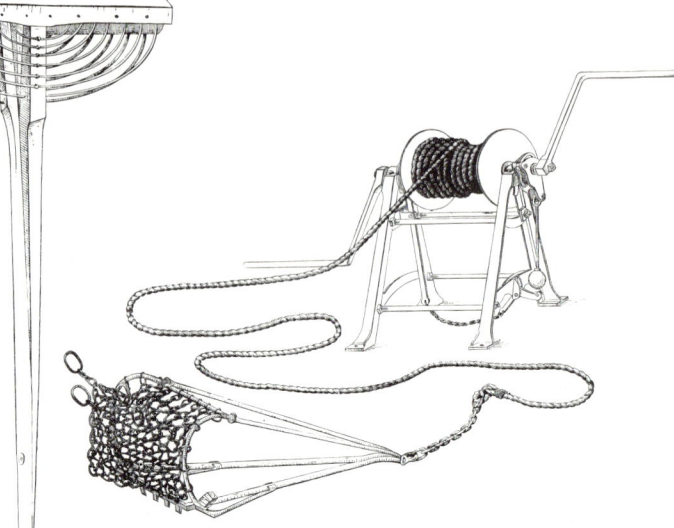

Chesapeake Bay Oyster Dredge

Oyster Tongs and Nippers

Dredging for Oysters, 1883

"Culling" in the Shop   Turnabout Dock, Patchogue   "Culling" on Board
Oystering on Long Island—Drawn by F. Dielman 1886

with rope meshing and chain links which hold the catch. The dredge is dragged over the oyster grounds in a fashion not unlike plowing and is then lifted to the boat by manual or mechanical means. Suction dredges are also employed and are very efficient in carrying oysters and other materials up from the bottom to the conveyor on the deck of the dredge boat. The suction dredge, in addition to harvesting oysters, helps clear the beds of starfish, drills, mussels, and other enemies of the oyster.

Two other methods of oyster harvesting, a shallow-water method employing a scoop-type harvester and a modern method employing human divers, produce relatively low numbers of oysters compared to the total industry harvest, but each is very efficient and may become more important as the industry continues to advance.

Once oysters are brought on board the vessel, they are "culled," or knocked apart with an iron hammer called a culling iron. Debris, empty shells, and bits of trash used to be thrown back into the water but now are put on the docks or planted off the grounds. The culled oysters are then separated into piles called cullings, mediums, or primes. Sometimes oysters are fattened on floats prior to bagging, though the practice is not as commonplace as it once was as a result of inshore pollution.

Ready for market, the oysters are bagged and tagged with a state identification tag and then transported by truck to major wholesale markets, retail operations, and processing houses. In former times, however, the process was more involved, and the cargo was brought by special "runner vessels" or "scows" to the wharves of major markets or shucking houses, off-loaded, and dumped into baskets, sacks, or bags by a special group of workmen known as the "scowgang."

During the mid and late 1800's one of the major markets in the country was to be found in New York City. The city

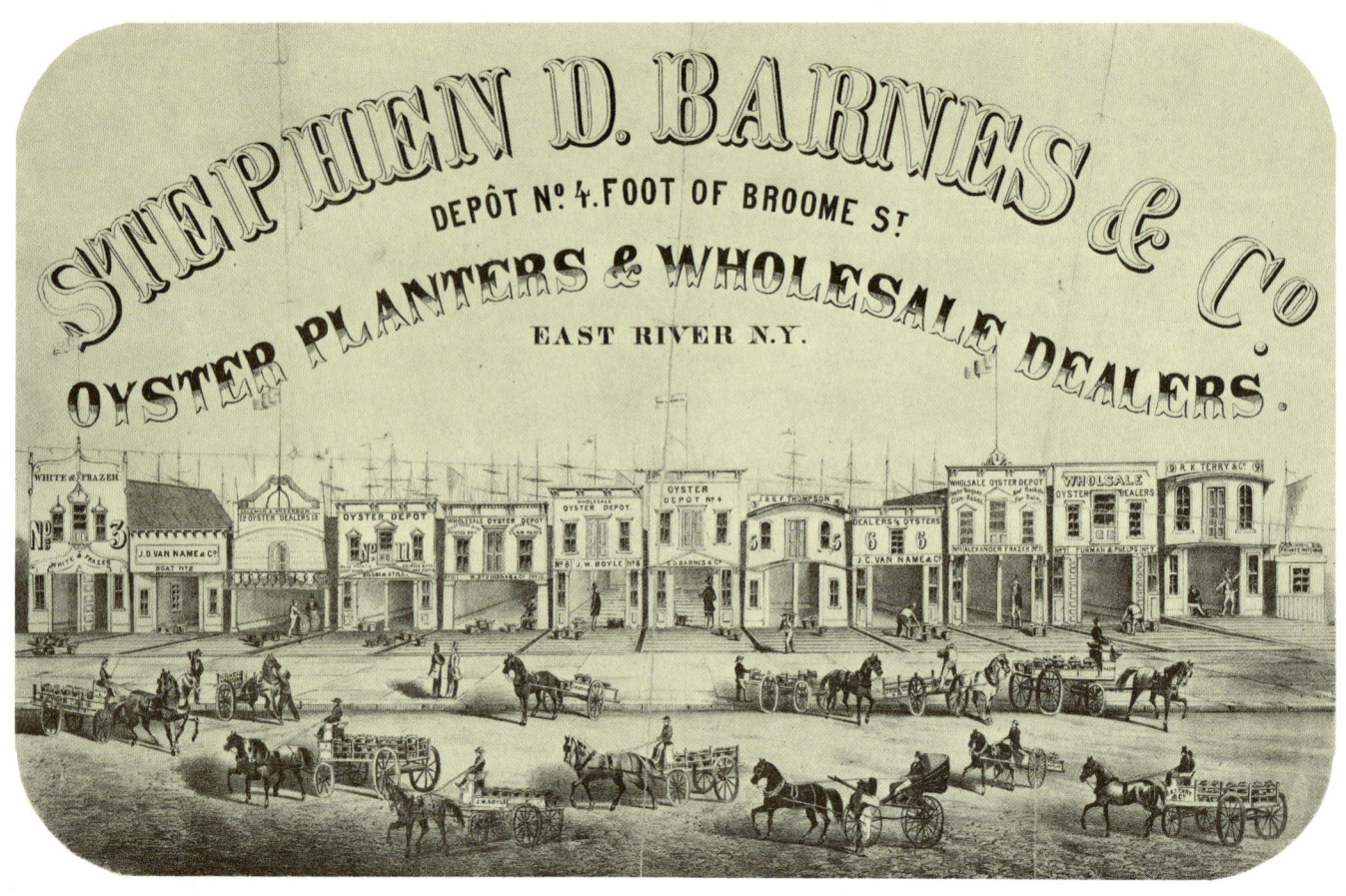

Oyster dealers of East River, New York City and their "arks." Masts of the oyster fleet can be seen in the rear and delivery wagons are busily engaged in the front. 1890's. Courtesy of the New York Historical Society.

market was a clearing-house for this most delightful yield of the sea. At water's edge, dealers occupied floating places of business known as scows, oyster boats, barges, or "arks." These craft were flat-bottomed boats approximately 24 feet wide and 75 feet long. Over the whole craft, and flush with the outside, a two story high house was built. The arks appeared, with the exception of their flat roofs, to closely resemble conventional picture-book impressions of Noah's ark, but they were securely fastened to the wharf or city water-wall and could be reached from the street by broad swinging platforms or plank sidewalks which allowed them to rise and fall with the tide. The rear or water ends of the arks were open to the boats and sloops which brought the oysters to the dealers.

The hold of the ark was divided into a number of compartments for the reception of the different varieties and sizes of oysters. The hold was well floored and served as a cellar, cool in the summer and warm in the winter. The floor of the first story was the deck of the ark and served as the general business compartment. Here, business transactions were concluded and oysters were opened, and the additional space was used for the storage of stock. When purchasers could be found immediately, the boats were off-loaded at one end and the baskets carried directly through the ark to the front door and thence to the long line of trucks or wagons which quickly drove them away to the restaurants and hotels in the city.

An office and sometimes living quarters were located on the second floor. In addition, barrels, baskets, and machinery were stored there. In every case, facing the wharf, a narrow balcony with a tiny roof could be found embellished with scrolls and patterns of quaint woodwork.

The daily capacity of these New York arks was about 700 bushels of oysters and the vessels, crowding along the entire length of the pier, handled on the average twenty five to thirty thousand baskets, or somewhat over 6,000,000 oysters a day. As can be imagined, the area was a center of activity with boats arriving constantly, men filling baskets or opening oysters, wagons and horses rolling over wooden docks or cobblestone streets, and oyster dealers anxiously trying to conduct some sort of civilized business. The oyster industry was becoming organized, and all along the Eastern coast, dealers were beginning to expand their operations and specialize in response to the increased demand for the oyster.

Those operations that primarily opened oysters came to be known as oyster shucking or opening houses, shops, or plants. Some of the larger shucking plants were equipped for packing and canning and as business boomed, oysters were packed in kegs, tubs, pails, and barrels for shipment inland. It was not only the seaport towns where oysters were eaten in enormous quantities, but towns a thousand miles from saltwater such as Cincinnati and St. Louis were regularly and abundantly supplied with oysters. Demand for the luscious bivalve caused the development of a curious system of supply long before the railways had stretched out their tracks to those distant regions. Mr. Maltby, a native of Connecticut, opened an oyster packing house in Baltimore and as business increased, he established a line of wagons to transport his oysters from Baltimore to Pittsburgh and points west. Maltby's "oyster express" employed light vehicles and fast drivers who drove through the night and changed horses two or three times a day. The "oyster express" was said to have been faster than the Government mails. Oysters were embedded in straw which was kept moistened by salt water. At Pittsburgh, the oysters were put on a swift boat for shipment west. As transportation methods improved, trains, and later trucks were employed to transport the oysters.

Dealing in oysters was a very lucrative

The principal storehouses, opening shops and packing house of H. C. Rowe & Co., of Fair Haven, Connecticut, built in 1885. From H. C. Rowe & Co. brochure.   Courtesy of Mystic Seaport Museum

business from the start and many oyster dealers made fortunes from the trade. Among the most well known oyster dealers were George Still, J & W Elsworth Co., the Merrell-Haviland Oyster Company, W.C. Porth and his brand of "Certified Oysters" and one of the oldest dealers, the Housemans. All of them worked out of New York City, but other dealers, including H.C. Rowe & Co. of New Haven, Connecticut, probably the wealthiest dealer of all, established themselves along the entire northeastern coast and Chesapeake Bay area. F. Mansfield & Sons of New Haven, Conn., the R.R. Higgins Co. of Boston, the Robert Pettis Co. of Providence, Rhode Island, and Mallory's "Diamond Brand" and Platt and Co. both of Baltimore, Maryland, were among the most important.

In the 19th century, the American people were enveloped in a "great oyster craze". No evening of pleasure was complete without oysters; no host worthy of the name failed to serve "the luscious bivalves," as they were actually called, to his guests. In every town there were oyster parlors, oyster cellars, oyster saloons, and oyster bars, houses, stalls and lunchrooms. Such operations did not originate in the United States but the popularity and originality of their presentation made them a unique American institution.

The oyster restaurant did not begin with the late nineteenth century oyster parlors, however. From all indications, no one in this country, other than the bargemen themselves, had thought of serving oysters to the public until 1763, when a primitive saloon was opened in New York City in a Broad Street cellar. "Half-shells were mostly called for then, for a stew was very expensive, and the fancy styles unknown. The oystermen most pleasantly remembered by old New-Yorkers are Sandy Welsh, John Dean, and Downing of Broad Street. Mr. Stringham, the partner in the oyster business of Mr. Blackford, the famous fish dealer at Fulton Market, was engaged in an oyster-house in Nassau Street, near the old Park

"Bon-Ton below stairs" or noisy revelry in a 19th century oyster cellar.

> "Let us royster with the oyster—in the shorter days and moister,
> That are brought by brown September, with its roguish final R;
> For breakfast or for supper, on the under shell or upper,
> Of dishes he's the daisy, and of shell-fish he's the star.
> We try him as they fry him, and even as they pie him;
> We're partial to him luscious in a roast;
> We boil and broil him, we vinegar-and-oil-him,
> And O he is delicious stewed with toast.
> We eat him with tomatoes, and the salad with potatoes,
> Nor look him o'er with horror when he follows the coleslaw;
> And neither does he fret us if he marches after lettuce
> And abreast of cayenne pepper when his majesty is raw.
> So welcome with September to the knife and glowing ember,
> Juicy darling of our dainties, dispossessor of the clam!
> To the oyster, then, a hoister, with him a royal royster
> We shall whoop it through the land of heathen jam."
> —*The Detroit Free Press*, Oct. 12, 1889

"Ain't this Oyster a very small one?"
"Small! why, no; it's only a little timid; that's all."

Theatre, some forty years ago. He says the great thing in those days was a shilling stew, and he remembers serving as many as five hundred of them a night."[8]

Operations which were run out of cellars became very common, although the establishments were not so much cellars as basements of commercial buildings and called "oyster saloons, parlors or bars" by owners.

An "oyster balloon" was displayed above each of the cellars or saloons which was "made of bright red muslin stretched over a global frame of wire, and illuminated at night by a candle placed within, the swinging crimson beacon serving to inform the hungry lover of the bivalve where he might procure them in every style, and in great perfection, as well as all the delicacies of the season, and all the drinks which American ingenuity has invented."[9]

To enter an oyster cellar, one had to go down a short flight of steps. They were usually 25 feet in width by a hundred or more in length, and many were handsomely fitted up with great luxury with tall mirrors and gold carved arcades, plate glass and gilded paintings, plush damask curtains, gleaming gas lights or splendid chandeliers, magnificent carpeting down the broad center aisle, and a resplendent bar at the end of the room.

Oysters, which due to their native element are more or less salt, were at one time sold as incitements to drink; they went by the cant terms of "shoeing horns," "gloves," or "pullers-on." So, as can be expected, the atmosphere in one of these crowded, all-male oyster cellars was one of excitement and noisy revelry described in those days as roystering.

One of the most popular and prestigious of the oyster cellars was Downings, at No. 5 Broad Street, which occupied the basement of two small buildings

8) "Harper's Weekly," September 9, 1882.

9) *Last Days of Knickerbocker Life in New York,* New York: G.P. Putnam's Sons, 1897, pp. 128-134.

Oyster Stalls and Lunch Rooms at Fulton Market, N.Y. *Frank Leslie's Illustrated Newspaper, 1867*

and was operated by a Negro proprietor. This cellar was "a popular gathering place because of its proximity to the Custom House (at Pine and Cedar Streets), the medium sized stores, the Merchant's Exchange, and the banks. Dayton recalled that leading politicians also made it their headquarters, dropping in to have a chat while enjoying their half-dozen Saddle Rocks or Blue Points. A host of men-about-town found time amid their varied duties, schemes, and pleasures to dive down the steep cellar steps to take a peep at Downing and have a few moments' cheerful chat. With such surroundings, Downing became a medium of communication from one customer to another, and it was rumored that he had great influence at City Hall. That drew many office-seekers as well as the regular patrons to the famous cellar which was open for oyster business at any time of the day."[10]

Such places came into immediate popularity. "They were places of resort for the politicians and public men of their time as some of the hotels and pretentious refectories are today. There the bewigged, powdered gentlemen of the early days met to drink the ale or beer that was provided, smoke their long-stemmed 'church-wardens' and discuss affairs of state".[11] It was not long before the oyster cellars, saloons, and parlors displaced the coffee houses and taverns as places of conviviality.

Witnessing the success and immense popularity of these oyster cellars and basement saloons, it was not long before enterprising entrepreneurs undertook similar operations above ground. The smaller of these operations, located generally in crowded centers or busy market areas, were called oyster stalls or refreshment stands and the larger, full-service restaurants became known as oyster houses and lunchrooms.

10) Meryle R. Evans, "Knickerbocker Hotels and Restaurants," *New York Historical Society Quarterly*, Vol. 36, No. 4, October 1952, p. 400.

11) "The Oysterman and Fisherman," February 4, 1916, p. 7.

The oyster houses and lunchrooms catered to the best class of people in the city and thousands of out of town people frequented them because they knew that they would get the choicest sea food, cooked and served in the best style. The consequence was that the amount of business done in these oyster houses was enormous. Frank Leslie, reporting on the scene in 1867, was especially struck by the crowds. "The rooms at certain hours of the day are crowded with eager customers, waiting for the first vacancy that offers. The situation of New York, obliging the larger part of the inhabitants to pass all day down town in business, and the nights up town at home, renders it necessary that a lunch of some kind should be taken during the middle of the day. Among the almost innumerable lunchrooms down town which seek to supply this demand, those about Fulton Market are as successful as any."[12] The excellence of the seafood presented in these establishments promoted and maintained their popularity. They were as distinctive in their way, according to Leslie, as the "up-town restaurants are in another."[13]

With the "express" service and the coming of the railroads, oyster houses developed and became prosperous inland, too. Pittsburgh, Chicago, and St. Louis boasted luxurious oyster houses with all the "mirrored marble and mahogany halls, elaborate styles of service, and accessories"[14] found in similar coastal establishments. These first class oyster houses were very probably "the source of more real enjoyment combined with a sufficiency of tone or style than any other class of public eating house."[15]

The greatest attention, however, in these oyster houses was given to their

12) "Frank Leslie's Illustrated News," May 18, 1867, p. 137.
13) "Frank Leslie's Illustrated News," May 18, 1867, p. 137.
14) Jessup Whitehead, *The Steward's Handbook*, 1893, p. 92.
15) Jessup Whitehead, *The Steward's Handbook*, 1893, p. 92.

Menu cover from a popular 19th century New York restaurant.

J.Y. Hart's Capital Oyster Saloon, St. Louis
Courtesy Missouri Historical Society

THE OYSTER STALL
"Penny a lot, Oysters! Penny a lot!"
(From a Daguerreotype by Beard)

specialty. Oysters were served in all styles, and the best cooks that money could procure were employed to present the luscious bivalve in "the most tempting forms." In addition, "they served fish of every saleable variety, shellfish such as lobsters, crabs, clams, crayfish, scallops, and the humbler mussel. Salads of all sorts, but more especially, fish salads, are made here to perfection. Very little attention is paid to the ordinary meat dishes of the restaurants, yet a steak or chop with potatoes can be had if any member of a party happens to have a distaste for fish foods."[16]

The popularity of the oyster and the quality of the seafoods served in the oyster houses insured the success of these establishments and carried them through the lean years of the Civil War. By 1874, over 850 oyster cellars, saloons, houses, and lunchrooms were located in New York City alone and their great popularity established them in other parts of the Eastern United States as well.

It was once said, and wisely too, that "you cannot eat the oyster in greater perfection that at a street stall, because, as the capital of the owner is small, so too is the stock; and to be sure of a rapid sale, it must also be well and carefully selected, and therefore does not need the announcement we read in many a byway one passes along, where 'the tale of a tub' would seem to contradict it: Oysters fresh every day."

The same wise commentator went on to remark, "The poor man has no need to bid his cook, like his wealthy neighbor, buy real salt water, or salts for the preparation of artificial seawater, for the preservation of his oysters. There are thousands of hands outstretched to receive his nimble penny, and to give him in return oysters as fine as any which can grace the table of the wealthiest in the land. To me it is a treat to stand by and see how rapidly oyster after oyster disappears down the capacious throat of some stalwart son of toil, and to think that my favourite health giving mollusk, in every one that is swallowed, is adding strength and muscle to those upon whom we so greatly depend for the nation's wealth and prosperity."[17]

Frank Leslie saw the cooks in these street stalls as the "objects of much curious conversation as they stir a fry in the iron pan, shake the tin can of the stews, and keep a pair of tongs poking between the oysters and the red-hot furnace bars on which they are roasted. In the busy part of the day the cook will be seen at any moment preparing the oysters in every possible form for the hungry folks outside, and if it is suggested that the heat of his fire must be very uncomfortable, he will simply give his shoulder

---

16) Jessup Whitehead, *The Steward's Handbook,* 1893, p. 92.

17) Philpots, *Oysters and All About Them,* John Richardson & Co., London, 1890, p. 280.

Oyster stands in the Fulton Market, a popular stop for shopping ladies. Harper's Weekly, *1870.*

a shrug and swing a pan of boiling bivalves and liquor about his head as if despising your limited knowledge of the great pride he has in being an A-1 Fulton Market Oysterman."[18]

In New York, the operators of these street stalls often served oysters on what was called the "Canal-street plan," which took its name from a wide street which crosses Broadway, on which the oyster stalls and street sellers abounded. This plan was to give a customer as many raw oysters as he could eat for sixpence. He paid his sixpence — York shilling, or Spanish eighth of a dollar — and swallowed the bivalves as they were opened, until he cried "enough!" The operation rarely lost money, however, for if they were plagued by an unreasonably greedy person, the dealers were in the habit of hurrying the exclamation by giving such a person, after he had got what the operator had estimated to be his money's worth, an unsavoury oyster to curb his appetite.

There was for a time something very like a mania for oysters in America and if pedestrians could not stop in at one of the oyster bars or houses that abounded in the cities in the 19th century, an obliging peddlar would fill their needs. This color-

18) "Frank Leslie's Illustrated News," February 17, 1877.

A Southern Oyster Peddler, 1889

ful character would make his rounds every morning and late afternoon. In 1889, a reporter for *Harper's Weekly* described one of the Baltimore street sellers: "He is faultlessly neat. His expansive white apron is his pride and his emblem. His sleeve coverings are second only to it in cleanliness. His large tin cans and his dipper and his measuring cup are radiant from polish. He himself is an irreclaimable old-timer. He has no sympathy with the modern specimens of his race; oftentimes they jeer at him, but he either ignores them or sends them back some cutting sarcasm that silences them. As he creeps up the street, his pace not being rapid enough for a walk, he lets the neighborhood know that he is around. He has a high, penetrating falsetto voice. It can be heard for a square or more, and many a late sleeper has criticised it with more emphasis than elegance. He has a variety of cries. One is 'oi-e,' uttered in a shrill pitch, with the explosion on the last syllable. Another is 'oi-oi-e,' which is a varied prolongation of the sound. When business is a little dull and time is plentiful he will indulge in the following, and throw into it all the picturesque resources of his vocal ability:

Here I have oysters to sell,
Oysters right fresh from the shell —
Oi-e!"

Counterparts of this type of person were to be found in all major coastal cities. Hand carts and horse-drawn wagons were introduced so the street seller's burden would be reduced and so he could service more customers.

In New York the character type was much the same and the oysterman cried with a grum and rough voice —

I've East River Oysters, suiting your choice;
Ye merchants or gentlemen, monks of the cloisters,
Have ye any such pleasure as eating of oysters?
They'll serve you for soup — or, fresh from the shell,
So nicely cut out, with relish as well,
Oysters! Oysters! friends will you buy 'em,
Were it not for your pleasure I never should cry 'em.[19]

Unfortunately, the oyster peddlar, like the 'ragman', the 'umbrella man', the 'knife and scissors man' and other colorful peddlars of the past century, has disappeared from modern society. Streets no longer ring with the shrill cries of men hawking prime, fat oysters for a penny, though even today many people remember and declare that they never had as delicious oysters as those procured from the street sellers or in the oyster houses.

19) *Cryes of New York,* early 1800's.

Serving an Oyster

Oyster lovers come from all walks of life from poor to wealthy, from the ordinary to the socially prominent. On two points, however, all connoisseurs are in agreement; oysters must be handled with respect and cleanliness is essential. As early as 1926, the U.S. Public Health Service, in cooperation with state and local governments as well as industry representatives, undertook a system of sanitary controls which would safeguard the public interest and the industry with regard to the purity of oysters. The waters in which the oyster beds are located are frequently inspected and analyzed, as are the oysters themselves, to insure that they are free of contaminents. Oyster growers and shippers operate under a system of permits and certificates which cover plant conditions and both the health and the ability of the workers who handle the oysters. Certificates indicating licenses and the place and date of harvesting accompany every shipment and provide protection from bootlegged stock. Canned, shucked oysters must be labeled with the proper State certifications number. Few foods are subjected to as rigid an inspection system as that imposed upon the oyster.

Oysters are often advertised on menus and in retail stores under the name of the locality in which they were grown. Well-known names, such as Blue Points, Chincoteagues, and Lynnhavens demand a higher price than their common compatriots from less fashionable neighborhoods. The consumer must, however, be constantly alert for unscrupulous or ignorant dealers who substitute cheaper oysters for the more popular brands and then charge the higher price. Deceptive shenanigans employed by dishonest dealers are difficult to detect, and the only way to insure against an inferior product is to rely upon and deal with a reputable merchant.

An oyster dealer testing a cargo, 1889

Fresh oysters may be purchased in three forms: live in the shell, shucked fresh and frozen, and canned. While frozen and canned oysters taste good, they do not compare well in flavor to the freshly shucked oyster, and the oyster liquor, so important to oyster lovers, is often lost in the preparations.

Oysters are a delicate and perishable meat. Purchased in the shell, they should be alive and kept under refrigeration. When the oyster is alive, the shell is tightly closed, although periodically oysters will open their shells and "breathe"; handling causes them to close up tight and those that remain gaping are probably dead and should be discarded as no longer useable. Spoiled oysters can also be detected by a slimy surface; by a strong, disagreeable, sulfurous odor

33

which may resemble that of a spoiled egg; or (if one is so unfortunate) by a harsh, metallic taste that will not soon be forgotten. This calls to mind the amusing story about Patrick, a servant boy in the 1800's, who blundered onto this gastronomical point. "He was told to go into the cellar and bring up some oysters in the shell; and his mistriss gave him a strict charge not to bring any that were dead. Patrick brought up a tray full, and every bivalve upon it was gaping wide! In reply to the astonished look of his mistress he said: 'Sure, Mam, they must be alive, or how could they keep their mouths open?' 'But, Patrick,' urged the lady, 'could you not tell the difference by the smell?' 'And sure, Mam, I was remarking that same to myself. But mightn't the others have bad breaths too, if they'd only open their mouths a bit?' Had the matter been pressed to an explanation, perhaps the mistress would have been as severely taxed as the servant to render a reason."[1]

Fresh shell stock, kept at 35°F, may be stored up to two weeks without creating a problem. Live oysters may be cooled in ice but should never be stored for any length of time in ice or potable water. Even though Federal Codes regulate the grades, sizes and counts of shell and shucked oysters, oystermen resist the standardization and continue to use traditional terms which vary from state to state and even among dealers. It would be advisable to ascertain from your dealer an explanation of the system in effect in your area. In general, oysters are sold by the barrel, the bushel, the gallon, the quart, the pint, or the dozen. The bushel basket is the standard unit of measure, though here, too, there is little uniformity; some dealers pack tightly and others do not.

In general, most oystermen recognize five grades of shell stock which correspond, more or less, to the size and age of the oysters involved:

"Run of the Rock" oysters are generally

Leslie's Magazine, 1913

considered a poor grade of haphazard, small oyster approximately two years old. These have been called at one time cullentines, seconds, or bushel oysters.

"Culls," or small oysters, are only slightly better than the lowly run-of-the-rock grade oysters. As the name implies, they are diminutive; and they are also young, ranging in age from two to three years. Culls come packed in bushels of about 350 and are commonly used in stews.

"Half-Shells" run about 225 to 300 per bushel and are considered superior oysters, ideal for raw service in restaurants or oyster bars. These oysters average two to four years in age and were formerly called Fancy or Bench oysters from the platform upon which they were opened.

"Mediums" are larger oysters about four

1) "Popular Science Monthly," November, 1874, p. 15.

to five years old, running about 175 to 200 per bushel. They are suitable for raw service or for frying.

"Box Oysters" are sometimes called large or "Extras" and range in age from four to ten years. They are such excellent frying oysters that the demand always exceeds the supply and rarely are they found in any but the best seafood restaurants or retail shops. The name originated in the practice of shipping large oysters in boxes instead of the typical barrels or sacks. Box oysters average 125 to 175 per bushel.

An oyster's meat can sometimes appear green, blue, brown, pink, or red in color, usually as a result of what the oyster has eaten, in combination with the temperatures to which the oyster has been subjected, both in the water and out. Such colorful oysters are generally safe to eat (although some of us avoid eating anything that is *generally* safe), but they are not as appetizing as the standard white or grey-white variety. Of course, any questionable oyster should be returned to the supplier or discarded.

Oysters can be eaten throughout the year, though traditionally they are most popular in those months possessing the letter 'r'; oysters harvested in

> "Those four sad months wherein is mute
> That one mysterious letter that has power
> To call the oyster from the vasty deep,"

(that is May, June, July and August) were considered unwholesome and even poisonous. Traditions of this nature often develop in response to human experience or perceived truths. In time, however, the reason for the existence of the traditions become obscure and invalid, and the persistence of the traditions themselves deprives us of pleasure unnecessarily. The ideas or notions pertaining to the proper time to eat oysters seem to have originated in olden times, though there is serious doubt that prehistoric man

"Oh! Bivalve. I fear those Cannibals are after us."
"Do not fear Shelly Dear we're safe there is no R in this month."

deprived himself of the most succulent product of the sea to satisfy the superstitions and fashions of civilized society.

The Grand Masters and Knights during the reign of the Order of St. John of Jerusalem were forbidden to eat oysters during the summer months but, the R canon, as it came to be known, gained full momentum and became entrenched in the 18th and 19th centuries. By the 1900's, poems, limericks, and illustrations had firmly established the custom of abstaining from oysters during the R-less months.

How did such ideas become so widespread? One possible reason for the tradition is that the R-less months coincide with the late spring and early summer breeding season of the oysters. During this time, an oyster appears somewhat "milky" and the flesh becomes thin, watery, and much depleted after spawning. The oysters remain in this condition until the fall or winter when they regain their plump size. In some areas of the country, oysters are protected by law during the R-less months, as a conservation method, and are allowed to breed undisturbed. This break also allows the oysterman to tend his beds, seed his crop and prepare for the next harvest.

Another reason suggested for the R canon is that the oysters are easily spoiled if kept out of water in hot weather. In the days before modern refrigeration, of course, many oysters undoubtedly spoiled before they came to market and it is likely that people who ate them became sick and thought themselves poisoned. Modern transportation and refrigeration, however, have virtually eliminated spoilage due to even the hottest weather, and today oysters can be safely purchased year round, though they become most plentiful in the market in the fall and winter months.

In general, it can be stated that oysters are, in their depleted state after breeding, not especially flavorful between the R-less months of May and August; nevertheless, the oyster is a wholesome food throughout the year. From a gastronomical point of view, therefore, the R canon should be discarded in the fashion W.E. Farbstein recommends—

"Many oyster lovers feel,
And very reasonably so,
That congress should at once repeal
The names of months that do not show
The letter R- and vote in lieu
Another group of means that do!"

Shucking is a term applied of course to the removal of the oyster meat from the shell. Shucked oysters should be plump and have a natural cream color with a grey or brownish tinge, depending on the locality from which they were harvested. They should produce a clear liquor, and be free of sand, silt, or shell particles. Shucked oysters are frequently washed, skimmed, and allowed to 'fatten' or bloat in water, and the wary buyer should be aware of the processes that are taking place. The fattening results as the meat becomes water soaked and swells; the natural salt liquid is displaced by fresh water and, within time, the oysters become flavorless and bleached white.

Freshly shucked oysters are sold (with the liquor) by the dozen or the pint. Canned or frozen oysters should be 'solid pack' and practically free of liquid, although some liquid will remain on the top and can be used for flavoring. Shucked oysters should be stored at 35°F or below and used within a week. Shucked oysters may be frozen in their own juice in freezer-resistant containers. The freezing of cooked oysters breaded or in other cooked dishes is preferable to the freezing of raw oysters, however. When freezing raw oysters in their own liquor, sufficient space must be left in the container to allow for the expansion of the liquid. Frozen oysters, stored at 0°F, may be held for three to six months. They should not be thawed until ready to use and once thawed, should never be refrozen. Shucked oysters may be purchased according to four size categories:

- Standards, which come packed approximately 400 to a gallon container, are generally used for stews or filling.
- Selects, which are also used for stews but which may be served raw, come packed 250 to 300 per gallon.
- Extra-Selects, which can be eaten raw but which are more commonly fried, come packed 200 to 250 per gallon.
- Counts, which are packed not more than 150 per gallon, are best suited for frying.

Experience and knowledge of eating habits of one's guests should determine the exact quantities of oysters to order, but as a general rule of thumb, three dozen shell oysters or one quart of shucked oysters should be sufficient for every six persons.

Opening oysters is an art and old timers easily amaze the uninitiated with their speed and skill.

Every fine hotel and grand restaurant (in addition, of course, to all the oyster houses) employed, in the days of the oyster craze, an oysterman whose job it was to prepare oysters and other shellfish for raw service. A good oyster shucker could easily manage to attend to his

Shuckers at Work—The Oyster Industry of Norfolk, Virginia, 1885

customers' voracious appetites, while providing them with a complimentary floorshow. "No other activity in the oyster business attracts so much interest as the dextrous movements of the oyster shucker. His skill, sharpened by thousands of openings, enables him to shuck one in a few seconds."[2]

The oyster shucking houses of the past century were hardly different than those in operation today. Standing in raised box stands to protect feet and clothing from seawater, liquor, and mud, shuckers quickly open the bivalves and flick them into stainless steel buckets according to size. Empty shells are discarded and soon form piles near the shuckers. While the operation may look easy, it is hard work, and according to Mr. Reed of Reed & Reed Oyster Company, Bivalve, New Jersey, only the fastest workers can open as many as ten gallons of oysters in an eight hour day. The shucked oysters are then skimmed, removing silt and shell particles, and put into coolers or cans to await shipment or sale. Shucking is an old and skilled occupation, but as a result of the drudgery associated with the labor, it is begging for apprentices and even though the job seems fairly secure, it would not be inappropriate to suggest that the oysterman or shucker works at an occupation in danger of extinction.

Anyone who has attempted to open shell oysters can easily appreciate the difficulties and arduous task of the professional shucker. The reluctant bivalve is a formidable obstacle and struggles valiantly with all who attempt to extricate him from his suit of shelly armor. The adductor muscle draws the shells tightly together with such force as to render the

2) John M. Kochiss, *Oystering From New York to Boston*, published for Mystic Seaport Inc. by Wesleyan University Press, 1974, p. 66.

37

"The First Day of Oysters" by G. Smith and G. Greatbach

mollusk impossible to pry apart. In an effort to overcome the beast's defenses, people have been known to attack it with hammers, pincers, stones, and similar objects. There have been a number of attempts to develop machines to open oysters and thus spare the pain and labor associated with the chore, but none have achieved any degree of success because of the varied shapes and thicknesses of the shells. Even in the 1800's when oysters were fashionable and everyone ate them, there was "scarcely one man in a thousand who knew how to open oysters."[3] The "true lover of an oyster should have some feeling for his little favourite, and patronize establishments only where they contrive to open them so dextrously that the mollusk is hardly conscious he has been removed from his lodging." That is, "till he feels the teeth of the piscivorous gourmet tickling him to death."[4]

For those persons who would appreciate the oyster in all its freshest glory, it would be well worth a little practice to learn to open the oyster oneself. When opening oysters, the proper equipment is essential. It has been said that a man may as easily open an oyster without a knife as a lawyer's mouth without a fee. Fingers are easily cut on the thin edges and the hard irregular shell of the oyster, and even experienced shuckers are not immune to painful wounds when the knife slips. Thick, coarse, woolen, rubber, or leather 'cots' as well as towels and finger stalls have been used to protect the hands while holding oysters to be shucked. An apron, a suitable knife, and a bench or platform to work on are the only other items a shucker needs to go into business.

3) *The Oyster Epicure (A Collation of Authorities on the Gastronomy and Dietetics of the Oyster),* White, Stokes & Allen, New York, 1883; quotation attributed to J.G. Wood, p. 7.

4) *The Oyster Epicure (A Collation of Authorities on the Gastronomy and Dietetics of the Oyster),* White, Stokes & Allen, New York, 1883, quotation attributed to *Murrey's Valuable Cooking Receipts,* p. 8.

> What is rough without, smooth within?
> Take something hard to enter in.
> When it is in, wiggle about,
> That's what makes the juice come out.
> —*Zook's Oyster House, Elverson, Pa.*

The method of opening oysters often depends upon the geographical location of the restaurant or market and the use for the shucked meats. There are as many varieties of shucking tools and implements as there are oysters, and each market has its own favorite. New York, New England, and the Chesapeake have developed techniques which have come to be traditional to the respective areas. During the last century, these traditional methods prevailed, but today, because of the scarcity of the shuckers, more than one method is likely to be seen in any given restaurant or oyster house.

Oyster Knife—"Shell out I say."
Oyster—"Oh! I thought there was no R in this month and I've only just come from my bed."

Carvel Hall
CRISFIELD, MARYLAND 21817

GREAT BLADES — Carvel Hall — SINCE 1895

Preferred since 1895 by canneries, hotels, restaurants, bar and seafood workers, Carvel Hall Oyster Knives are designed by professional oyster openers and made in "Oyster Country" by craftsmen with years of experience in making oyster knives for expert seafood workers.

Carvel Hall Oyster Knives are precisely weighted and sized. Rugged yet flexible blades of high carbon steel are expertly ground, oil tempered and then permanently locked in correctly shaped hardwood handles.

R. MURPHY KNIVES
STAY SHARP 1850 — MADE SHARP AND STAY SHARP
Ayer, Massachusetts 01432

R. Murphy Shellfish knives are the recognized leaders for the industry. Made with the finest cutlery steel, blades are uniformly hardened and taper ground . . . guaranteed not to break. Many styles are offered for varying shell forms . . . most are available in stainless as well as high carbon steel. Handles are shaped to provide leverage and solid grip for the shucker working for long hours with wet hands.

CHESAPEAKE STABBER
Long narrow blade is precisely tempered for strength and resiliency. Tested among professional shuckers and enthusiastically acclaimed.

CRACK KNIFE
One piece, all steel construction provides extra "cracking" weight ideally suited for use with "wild" or "clustered" oysters.

NEW HAVEN
Stubby, wide bladed knives. Preferred in New England but popular everywhere.

SOUTHERN AND GALVESTON
Designed for use in southern and Gulf Coast regions. Special new double hollow grind for easier penetration and faster cutting.

"The Oyster Shanty" by Henry J. Peck, 1908

In general, when preparing oysters for raw service, the shuckers should beforehand examine them and remove any dead or unsuitable stock. Usable oysters may be scrubbed and washed to remove the silt and debris usually found on the outer shells. Then they should be chilled on ice or in a cooler, with provisions made to allow adequate drainage. Oysters must never be allowed to soak in water. To prevent 'tightening-up' the oysters should be handled as little as possible. The technique employed should produce a whole meat, free from unsightly incisions and shell particles, in as swift and natural a motion as possible. Every effort should be made to save the juice or liquor, and the oyster should not be washed once it is opened lest this natural flavor be lost. The most successful method, however, is the one which works best for the individual's specific needs. The following illustrations and procedures describe the four most commonly employed opening techniques for raw service.

Once the succulent bivalve has been successfully extracted from its shell, our attentions turn to the proper methods of serving. Oysters may be served on either the flat shell or the deep hollow half. Both methods have particular advantages. The oyster served on the flat shell appears

The Stabbing or Sticker Method

Care must be taken when using this technique to avoid slipping and stabbing the palm or wrist. With practice, this is a very simple technique and not as strenuous as some of the other methods.

With the left hand, the shucker braces the oyster on a non-slip surface with the flat side up and the "mouth" or widest end of the shell facing the opener. The hinged end is usually wedged against a wooden cleat or stop.

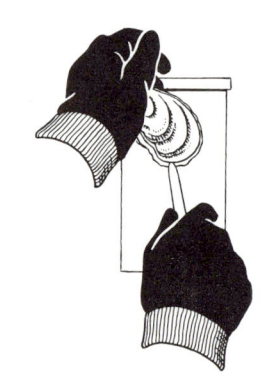

Constantly wiggling the stabber with short clockwise and counter-clockwise twists of the wrist, the shucker works the point of the knife, angled down, between and into the shell. Sometimes more than one try is necessary to gain entry.

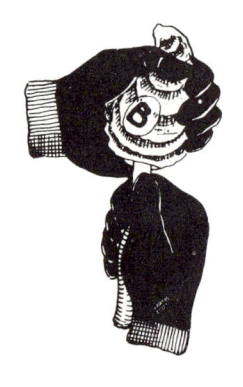

He pushes the blade straight in, wiggling the oyster sideways with the left hand until he has cut the muscle (B) and the shell has released to the point where he can pry it open with the knife.

He turns the oyster over in the same motion and cuts the muscle on the remaining half-shell, removing any silt or shell particles with the knife before serving.

The Cracker Method

(also referred to as cracking, billing, or breaking)

In this method, a block of wood or iron rail with a flat upper surface about two inches long by one inch high by 1/4 inch thick, called a cracking iron, is employed as well as a hammer.

The shucker grasps the oyster in the palm of his left hand, (deep shell down, flat shell up), the oyster knife and hammer held in his right hand to save time. He holds the knife firmly, but with some flexibility to permit ease of handling and at least some protection should the knife slip.

He places the edge of the shell on the block, extending over the 'cracking iron' and breaks off the 'bill' at the thin end (the growing edge) of the shell with a sharp rap of the hammer

and inserts the knife in the opening where the shell was broken. He slides the knife between the oyster meat and the shell and wiggles the oyster back and forth in his left hand, continuing until the adductor muscle or "eye" (B) is cut and the shell loosens. He then pries the upper shell off by using the blade as a lever, removes any silt or shell particles with the knife,

and severs the muscle of the oyster on the remaining half-shell. The oyster is now ready to serve.

The Hinge Method

This method usually requires a considerable amount of pressure and for this reason is generally less suitable in restaurants and oyster shucking houses. The New Haven knife is best suited for this method.

The shucker grasps the "mouth" or widest end of the oyster in the palm of his left hand using a towel for additional protection and breaks the ligament or hinge of the oyster by pressing the point of the knife into the center of the black mass between the upper and lower shells.

When he presses down on the knife, the lid or upper shell should pop open for him and allow him to cut the muscle from the upper shell by sliding the knife, curved tip down, between the shell and the meat.

He can then remove the silt and shell particles with the knife, cut the muscle (D) on the lower shell, as a convenience to the guests, and serve.

The Side Knife Method

This is a difficult maneuver to master, but once learned it is well suited for raw service. The New Haven oyster knife works best with this technique.

The shucker who uses the side knife method grasps the oyster in the palm of his left hand with the deep shell down. He holds the knife with his thumb extended on the blade to within 1/4 inch of the point, the curved tip facing downward, places the point of the knife on the inside of the outer edge of the upper shell, and wiggles the knife down and between the shells.

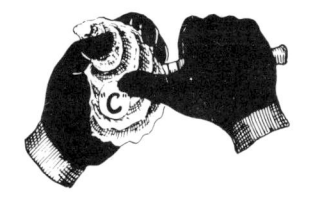

He then pushes the blade across and under the upper shell and cuts the muscle at (C), in the third diagram above, using care to avoid cutting or damaging the flesh which would result in watering and the loss of the oyster's plumpness. He keeps his thumb on the oyster and pries the shell off, removing silt and shell particles that may appear on the meat.

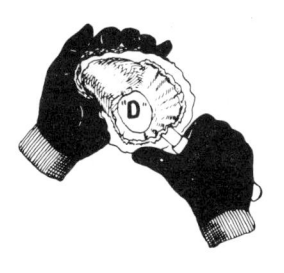

Then he turns the blade curved tip up and cuts the muscle (D) on the lower shell. The oyster is then ready to serve.

Shucking Procedures Courtesy Bluepoints Co., Inc. and Parks' Seafood, Inc.

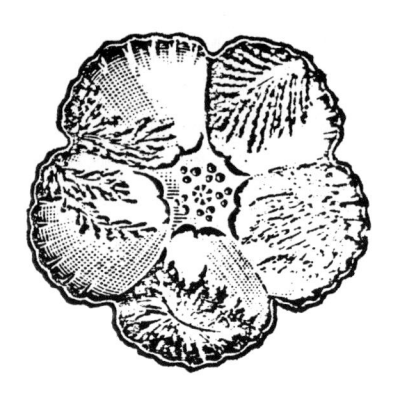

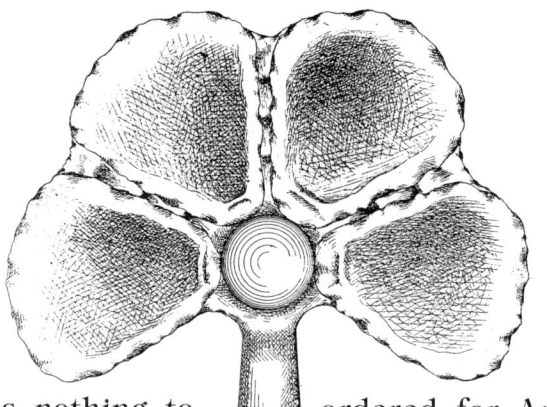

more plump, but there is nothing to prevent the precious liquor or "oyster broth" from draining away, and more gourmets insist that the mollusk be served in all its glorious brine upon the deep shell. Others prefer that the bivalve be "bearded"—that is, removed of its gills prior to service, though this operation is not very widespread or popular.

Oysters which have been prepared for raw service as appetizers on the half shell are usually served upon a bed of cracked ice in chilled, deep bowls or plates especially suited for the purpose. These plates are set upon a somewhat larger "place plate" in order to protect the table should the ice melt and overflow. At the end of the course, the used plate is removed, leaving the place plate. When oyster soup is served, the soup plates are usually warmed in advance and upon conclusion of the course, the soup plate and the underlining plate are removed. Oysters served on the half shell may be placed at each cover or setting before the meal, but it is better to serve them just before the guests are seated.

The "great oyster craze" had considerable influence upon the economy and eating habits of people in the 19th century, and one of the most unique and unusual developments was the appearance and sudden popularity of the oyster plate. These plates were highly ornate and decorated with fancy gold lace borders, scroll work, and flowers of delicate tints. They invariably had receptacles made to resemble the interiors of oyster shells. Most of the plates were ordered for American use by famous china distributors whose names were marked on the back of the plates, and they could frequently be found in the butler pantries and dining rooms of the affluent during the Victorian era.

As the oyster beds were rapidly but quietly becoming depleted by the end of the 19th century, and the bivalve becoming ever more fashionable, the popularity of the plate, too, seemed to reach a peak between 1880 and 1900. The reason for their origin is uncertain, though there is a good possibility they were introduced as glamorous specialty china and perhaps even to keep the dirty shells out of the proper Victorian dining rooms. Whatever the case may be, they were popular and remained in vogue for a considerable period of time, and they serve now as lovely decorations in many of the finest oyster restaurants.

Oyster plates were, in many instances, hand painted and custom made. They varied considerably in shape, in color, and in the number of receptacles for the oysters. They were most commonly found with four to six receptacles and a deep center well which was once used to accommodate a wedge of lemon but more recently a container of cocktail sauce. The plates were divided into three distinct groups or types: the deep dish bowl, the welled-plate with small indentations imitating oyster half-shells, and the deep-welled plates designed for serving individual oysters on their own. The deep dishes or bowls were filled with crushed ice and the oysters were arranged like

(1)
Deep dish

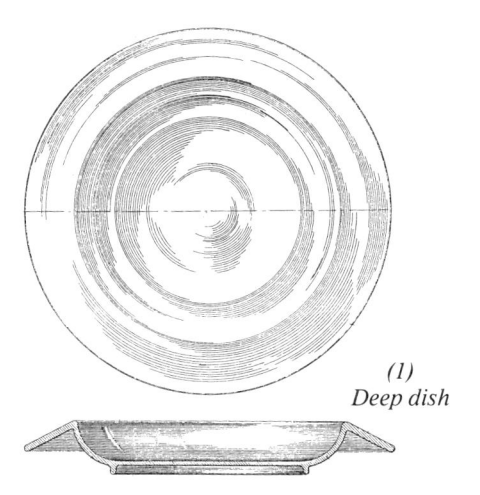

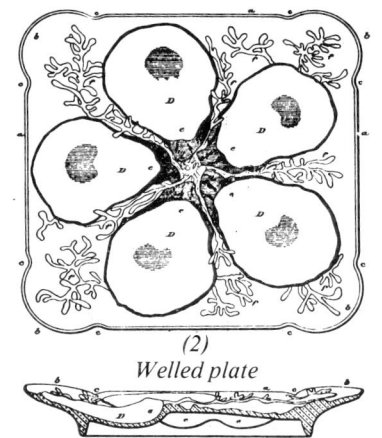

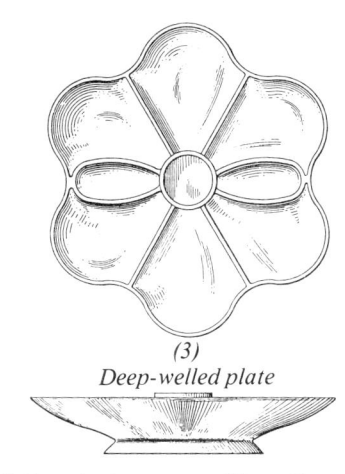

(2)
Welled plate

(3)
Deep-welled plate

spokes of a wheel about the center which contained the rounded shell or a container of sauce. It is difficult, if not impossible, to discern between the bowl which is intended for soup and that which was designed for the service of oysters and, in fact, they were often used interchangeably. The welled-plates were primarily used as show pieces and prestige items. One such plate was custom-made for President Rutherford B. Hayes for regular use in state functions. These plates, however, were seldom used in restaurants or hotels because of their cost, and because their unusual forms did not allow easy stacking, washing and drying. Manufacturing of the plates all but ceased in the early 1900's and they are valued today primarily as collectors items and heirlooms.[5] While custom-made oyster plates are not essential for the service of raw oysters, there can be little doubt as to their ability to enhance the presentation and create a memorable experience.

Raw oysters are thought by many to be most enjoyable when held with the fingers and supped from the shell; though, quite properly, they are often served with a fork designed specifically for cocktail service. This utensil is referred to as an oyster, cocktail, or seafood fork and (should there be any doubt) it is usually the smallest fork in the place setting. Oyster forks are slender, diminutive in form, and charmingly designed to efficiently skewer the delicate bivalve.

In final preparation for the service of oysters, it is essential that dishes and silver, including the oyster fork, be clean; linen or table surfaces, spotless; and the glasses sparkling and free from fingerprints or smudges. Containers of sauces, crackers, or other suitable condiments should be wiped clean and adequately filled prior to service. Lemons should be juicy and cut in sixths or eighths rather than slices which are more difficult to handle. Lintless, cloth napkins are much more appropriate than paper ones for this type of service. With these final preparations in order, the diner may get down to the more serious business of eating the oyster.

5) Although the exigencies of publishing a book such as this preclude an extensive display of color photographs of these remarkable pieces of American folk art, the serious student of the subject should make a point to see the large collections at both Parks' Seafood in Allentown, Pa., and the Sansom St. Oyster House in Philadelphia, Pa.

AN ELEMENT OF SOCIAL EXISTENCE

Of all the molluscous animals, the oyster is commercially the most important, and gastronomically it is the most delicious. Pliny, an ancient Roman chronicler, described oysters as "the palm and pleasure of the table". In its normal condition, the oyster is an excellent food, and it has been demonstrated as a gastronomic truth that there is no feast worthy of a connoisseur where oysters do not come to the front. "It is their office," said John Philpots in 1890, "to open the way, by that gentle excitement which prepares the stomach for its proper function, digestion; in a word, the oyster is the key to that paradise called appetite."[1] Ranked among shellfish, it is without a doubt the "Queen of the Bivalves".[2]

"The Oyster Eaters" L. Boilly, 1825

There are many advantages to serving oysters. They are refreshing and entirely edible, easily digested, and an excellent source of vitamins, minerals, and proteins. They are also highly regarded for their power to revive and stimulate a jaded appetite when taken in the "freshness of life". One feels a great sense of well-being after eating oysters, a feeling somehow not associated with any other food. It is not exactly a sense of repleteness, but, as John Runyon said, a "strange ethereal sensation as though one had supped off fairy food that whispered kindly and benignly to the digestion".[3] Oysters are quickly and easily prepared and there are a wide variety of cooking methods; they are easy to serve, which makes them especially useful for the hungry and tired on cold, wet evenings when nothing less than a quick, heartening meal will suffice. There is an interesting story about Benjamin Franklin during one of his sojourns in the New England states. It was rather late in the evening and the chill air aggravated the arthritis-ridden bones of the weary

---

1) Philpots, *Oysters and All About Them,* John Richardson & Co., London, 1890, p. 313.
2) "Popular Science Monthly," November, 1874, p. 172.
3) John Rydon, *Oysters with Love,* Peter Owen Ltd., London, 1968, p. 99.

> ## How to Kill an Oyster
>
> Don't drown him in vinegar
> or season him at all,
> Don't cover up his shining form
> with pepper like a Pall,
> But gently lift him from his shell
> and firmly hold your breath,
> Then with your eager tongue and teeth
> just tickle him to death.
>
> —Chas. Krumling, 1910

traveler, so he decided to stop for the evening at a local inn. Unfortunately, as he entered, all the seats about the warm fire were occupied and none offered to relinquish his place. Dr. Franklin called upon the landlord to give his horse a bag of raw oysters. When the landlord hesitated at such an unusual request, Dr. Franklin repeated the order, insuring that all in the room would hear his instructions. The anxious landlord, wishing to satisfy every wish of his guest, despite the unusual nature of this particular one, carried the bag of oysters outside to the horse, accompanied by curious spectators who had been seated by the fire. Soon the landlord returned and told the doctor, who was now seated in the warmest spot by the fire, that the horse refused the oysters. Dr. Franklin replied, "Poor, foolish beast! He does not know what is good; bring them to me and see if I refuse them!"

Taste is every person's private laboratory and while there are few absolutes regarding culinary preparation and consumption of food, epicures, gourmets, and authorities of food seem to be in agreement that some methods of eating oysters are preferable to others. The ancients, our teachers in all arts, but especially in aesthetics, did not bolt the oyster, but masticated it. With true epicurean tact, they always extracted the full enjoyment out of the good things set before them. Dr. Kitchener, a 19th century epicure, recommended that "those who wish to enjoy this delicious restorative in its utmost perfection must eat it at the moment it is opened, with its own gravy in the undershell"; and that unless it is eaten while "absolutely alive" its "flavour and spirit are lost".[4] Eaten in its natural state, with its own liquor, the oyster has a much finer flavor than in any other form, and it is far more nourishing.

It is said that appetite grows upon what it feeds on, and there is no fixed rule with regard to the quantity of oysters that a person may eat. The second mouthful is usually more tempting than the first—the third surpasses the second, and so on and on. The amount of oysters to eat will vary with appetite, the nature of the event, and the generosity of the host.

History abounds in instances of the extraordinary capacity of man for the consumption of the oyster. The chroniclers tell that the Emperor Vitellius could eat a thousand of these bivalves at a meal. In those past ages of great excesses, peacock feathers were employed to act as throat ticklers so that the wealthy might regurgitate and thus be able to begin their effort to satisfy their enormous appetites anew. In later years, the dainty throat ticklers were abandoned but the numbers of oysters eaten by gourmands remained impressive.

Today, an average serving of oysters generally consists of a plate of 4, 5, or 6 oysters before dinner, though Mr. Whitehead reminds us that "fashion ever interferes in the matter".[5] It is certain too, that many living gourmands may agree with Baron Graham's observations after disposing of ten dozen oysters—"Something must be wrong with me! I have eaten 120 oysters and pon' my word and honor, I don't think I am quite as hungry as when I began."[6]

Whatever your preference may be concerning the amount of oysters to be eaten,

---

4) *The Oyster Epicure (A Collation of Authorities on the Gastronomy and Dietetics of the Oyster),* White, Stokes & Allen, New York, 1883, p. 7.
5) Joseph Whitehead, *Hotel Meat Cooking,* 1880.
6) *The Oyster Epicure (A Collation of Authorities on the Gastronomy and Dietetics of the Oyster),* White, Stokes & Allen, New York, 1883, p. 17.

AN OYSTER SUPPER *by N. Currier*
Courtesy of the Museum of the City of New York

they are to be best enjoyed, as we have repeated once or twice, when they are eaten in the natural juices without condiments of any sort. But if you will not eat your saline dainties naturally, then a little lemon juice is all that is necessary so that the delicacy of their flavor need not be lost. The oyster is, however, often served with cocktail or tartar sauce, vinegar, cayenne pepper, hot sauce, crackers, or brown bread and butter.

Though not altogether teetotalers, oysters do not favor strong drinks. Light wines, malt liquors, and ale are the more proper and seasonable accompaniments but personal preference must take priority with regards to the appropriate beverage. If a person appreciates a good red wine with fish, table etiquette or formality should not disallow or disapprove of his enjoyment. Nevertheless, as a general rule of thumb, some beverages are more acceptable to the digestion and are better suited to enhance the taste than others. With raw oysters, crisp, light, dry wines are usually drunk in preference to red wines. If the oysters are served in a sauce, the predominant flavor should determine the appropriate wine.

Chablis, characterized by the tart, flinty flavor of the Chardonnay grape, harmonizes well with the mineral rich, slightly metallic overtone of raw oysters. Pale, golden Muscadet has a delicate, floral aroma and a dry, light flavor and leaves a slightly musky aftertaste that will enhance any oyster dish.

Graves, a pale yellow, dry wine with a light, fruity bouquet, is a pleasant companion with fried oysters. Rhine wines and Moselles are also used successfully. Dry Sauternes and Barsacs are crisp, clean, and acidic enough to balance well with more complex oyster entrees. Smoked oysters taste best with a dry Sherry wine. Champagne, or any sparkling wine, with its small bubbles and dry fresh taste, is well balanced and traditionally blends well with most oyster dishes.

Of beer and other spirits, many are of divided opinion. Some disapprove entirely, while others are more qualitative in their judgment, and still others are in the habit of washing the oyster down with whatever liquid is at their disposal.

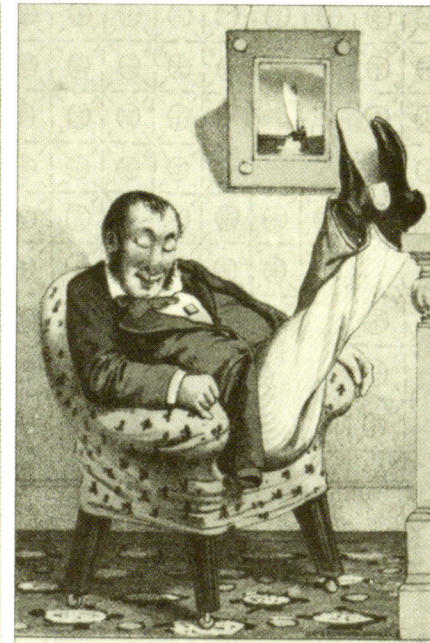

| Life is of little object with him if he cannot dine on the DIAMOND BRAND OYSTERS. He is getting so thin he is tempted to go and shoot himself. | He accidently discovers a place down town where they are kept for sale, immediately purchases some of them and concludes to live. | Exists on them for a week, regains his flesh, secures his accustomed snooze after dinner, and is once more a happy man, |

19th century trade card courtesy Mr. Frank Cagianese

When eating oysters on the half-shell, the shell is held or steadied with the left hand and the meat lifted whole with the oyster fork. Some prefer to sup or slurp the oyster directly from the shell lest the juice and flavor escape through the punctures caused by the tines of the fork. Whatever method is preferred, the oysters "floating in their own broth ought to be lifted quickly to the lips and eaten as soon after opening as possible before the delicate aroma has been dissipated into the atmosphere. There is as much difference between the oyster then opened and eaten as between champagne, frothing and leaping out of a silver-necked bottle, and the same wine after it has been allowed to stand for six hours with the cork removed."[7]

The oyster is usually eaten in one bite, and generally should not be cut. It is quite acceptable to pick up the shell after eating the oyster to drain the liquor into your mouth. This should be done gracefully by picking up the shell between the thumb and forefinger. "If a chip of shell should get into your mouth while eating, remove it unobstrusively."

History is replete with examples of the beneficial and stimulating effects the oyster has had on mankind. It has been praised as the "very perfection of the digestive ailment" and lauded by such as Casanova as "a spur to the spirit and to love". Doctors have prescribed the oyster as a universal remedy and romancers herald the bivalve as "the most effective of all seducers".[8] Indeed, few foods that have received the wide acceptance the oyster has received have been fortunate enough to also enjoy its passionate following.

A distinguished doctor of the last century asserted that "there is no alimentary substance, not even excepting bread, which does not produce indigestion under given circumstances, but oysters never. We may eat them today, tomorrow, eat them always, and in great profusion, without fear of indigestion."[9] Another stated that "when spirits are depressed, and disagreeable feelings pervade both

7) *The Oyster Epicure (A Collation of Authorities on the Gastronomy and Dietetics of the Oyster),* White, Stokes & Allen, New York, 1883, p. 18.

8) Robert Hendrickson, *Lewd Food,* Chilton Book Co., Radnor, Pa., 1974, p. 40.

9) Philpots, *Oysters and All About Them,* John Richardson & Co., London, 1890, p. 313.

the body and mind, in consequence of impaired digestion, let the persons so afflicted eat a few oysters, and cheerfulness soon returns. They are enabled once more to see through the gloom which seemed to envelop the system in a living shroud; the physical powers are renewed, and life once more seems sweet to the man who but a short time before wished life was at an end." A certain Doctor Leroy was in the habit of taking two dozen of these delicious fish every morning before breakfast, and when he had finished them, he would exultingly exhibit the empty shells to his friends, exclaiming with a smile, "There you may behold the fountain of my youthful strength."[10]

To understand the remarkable recuperative power of the tiny mollusk, it is necessary to analyze its chemical and nutritional composition. Few foods, from a dietetic standpoint, are better balanced nutritionally. In composition, oysters are very similar to milk and, with only a few additional calories, are self-sufficient as a diet. With the growing recognition of the importance of a balanced diet in safeguarding health, it is important to note that according to the American Dietetic Association, oysters are a low cholesterol food source. They contain glycogen, an easily digestible form of carbohydrate generally lacking in other foods. One cup of raw oysters has only 100 calories, yet a pound of this meat supplies 7% of the daily energy consumed by man and 28% of the necessary protein.

Although the precise reasons behind the healthful nature of the oyster remained hidden to the researchers and practitioners of the last century, on a practical level they realized, as they did about so many other substances, the beneficial effects of the oyster. "Living oysters are endowed with the proper medicinal virtues; they nourish wonderfully, and solicit rest; for he who on oysters sups, is wont on that night to sleep placidly; and to the valetudinarian afflicted with a weak stomach, oppressed with phlegm or bile, eight, ten, or twelve raw oysters in the morning, or one hour before dinner, is more healing than any drug or mixture that the apothecary can compound."[11] Mr. Philpots wrote in "Oysters and All About Them" that by taking oysters daily, even persons suffering from "almost incurable digestion, very soon find the most agreeable effects on the human kitchen and laboratory; its functions become regular, without the use of strong medicines. Depression of spirits and other disagreeable feelings consequent on impaired digestion soon cease to affect them; headaches disappear; and the heretofore dyspeptic, sour, unhappy tempered man, becomes a pleasant and joyous companion, full of life himself, and inspiring to those around him."

Oysters contain many vitamins essential to growth, vigor, and the maintenance of health as well as protein for building muscles and strong body tissue. Ample amounts of vitamin A, for resistance and for strengthening the eyes and the lungs; B for ease of digestion and appetite; C, which prevents tooth decay and promotes endurance and is found in only a few other meat products such as sweetbreads, liver, and heart; D, the sunshine vitamin; and G, which is essential for growth and counteracts nervous fatigue, are all to be found in the delicious oyster.

In mineral content, oysters are not found to be wanting in essentials. They contain almost one-half of the recommended daily allowance of iodine, which is necessary for healthy thyroids. Other minerals to be found in oysters include copper for the building of blood, calcium for the development, growth, and maintenance of bones and teeth, phosphorus, magnesium, thiamine, riboflavin, niacin, iron, and zinc.

But nutritional benefits derived from eating oysters is not the only reason prompting their great popularity. Belief in aphrodisiacs, and the prominent role of

10) Philpots, *Oysters and All About Them,* John Richardson & Co., London, 1890, p. 317.

11) "Harper's Weekly," March 16, 1872.

the oyster in this field, has undoubtedly tempted many an unwilling person to consume the delicate bivalve in the hope of stimulating some emotional response or reviving some dormant power.

Many world cultures have relied upon erotic stimulants and the use of aphrodisiacs is deeply rooted in our cultural past. Every imaginable means has been attempted to arouse or stimulate sexual desire, and oysters have played an especially prominent role in reducing the resistance to seduction or in improving performance once the initial resistance has been overcome.

The ancient Romans included oysters in their banquet menus, many of which degenerated into orgies, and there are frequent references to their employment among the "shameless and lascivious women" of the time. Byron wrote in "Don Juan" that "oysters are amatory food" and later, as if to verify the statement, Casanova, who generally ate fifty raw oysters before breakfast, commented that eating "so delicate a morsel must be a sin in itself."

Theodore, the king of Corsica, proclaimed his three great passions as being "love, military glory, and the oyster!" And it was rumored that Napoleon's military prowess was in some part due to his habit of dining upon the bivalves before every battle. Who can say how many battles and glorious 'charges' of yesteryear were inspired by the oyster?

The prolific reproductive processes and the general assumption that 'like breeds like' make the oyster a suitable aphrodisiac. The numerous young demonstrate conclusively its fertility, and would it not be reasonable then to assume that by eating the oyster one's own fertility might be improved? Others would point out the physical analogies between the oyster and the human genitalia and symbolic comparisons such as the pearl nestled in the soft interior of the opened shell cannot be overlooked. It has been said that the "first oyster eaten alive and on the shell is a kind of gastronomic loss of virginity."

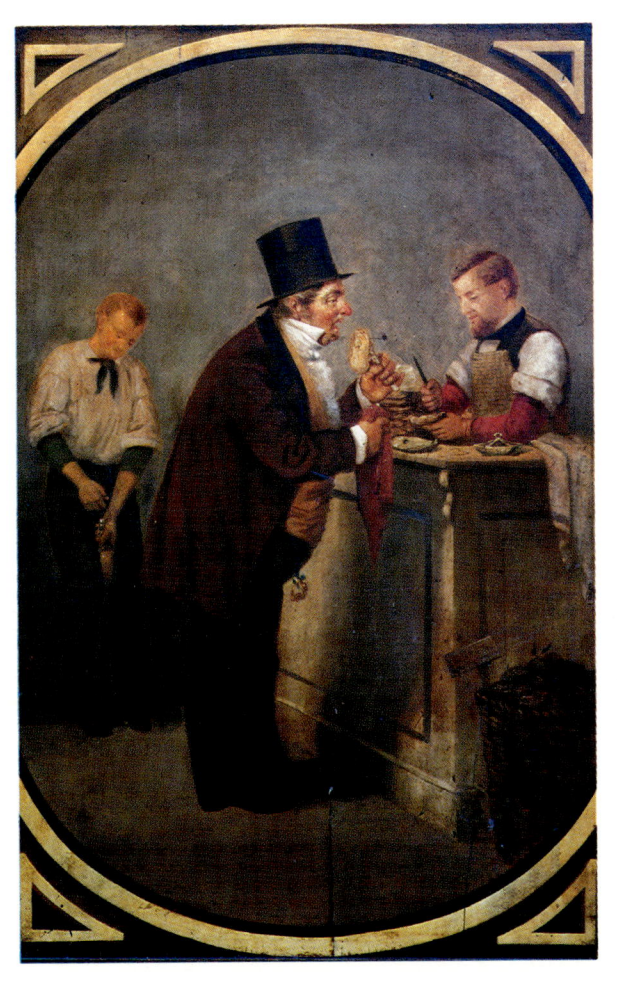

Original Oil Sign Painting courtesy of the Garden Restaurant, Philadelphia.

Whatever the case may be, oysters and love seem to naturally blend together. Oysters are a nourishing restorative and their consumption leads to a sense of well-being. There can be little doubt that oysters provide an ideal environment for lovers.

The recipes contained in this book give specific, kitchen tested instructions for cooking oysters. In general, shellfish should not be cooked long or at high temperatures lest they become tough and rubbery. Shells should be washed and scrubbed thoroughly before being used for cooking. When moist heat methods of cookery are employed, a more tender and flavorful product will be realized if they are simmered at 185-190°F rather than boiled. Oysters may be baked or roasted at 400°F for 10 to 15 minutes, or until they open. Three to five minutes should be sufficient time when deep-fat frying or pan-frying to turn the breading golden brown and to thoroughly cook the oyster itself.

Tom (*to Tim, who has just eaten an oyster*). "Well, Tim, how was it?"
Tim (*in ecstasy*). "The Oyster was fine, but the Winegar and Ketchup were hevingly!"

Parks' Oyster & Clam Bar Stew

    24 shucked oysters (6 to 8 per serving)
    1 cup oyster or clam liquor
    2 cups milk
    8 butter pats (2 per serving)
    ½ tsp celery salt
    ½ tsp ground white pepper
    Spanish paprika

Method—Remove any pieces of shell from the oysters and strain liquor. Reserve and combine with clam juice or broth, if necessary. In a separate pot scald milk or light cream to just below the boiling point. Melt half the butter in another pot. Add oysters and liquor and cook until the edges of the oysters curl slightly, approximately 3 minutes. Avoid overcooking the oysters or they will toughen. Add the scalded milk and season with celery salt and white pepper. Do not allow the stew to boil or the milk will curdle. Ladle into pre-warmed soup bowls; add remaining butter and garnish with paprika and chopped parsley. Serve at once while piping hot. Serves 4.

Accompaniments—oyster crackers, bread (brown or French) and butter, Worcestershire sauce.

Optional: Cayenne pepper, hot sauce, or Worcestershire sauce may be added to the stew.

Pan Stew

A variation of the Oyster House Stew. Substitute oyster liquor or clam broth for the milk and serve with toast points.

Boston Oyster Stew

Another regional variation of the Oyster House Stew. Substitute light cream or a mixture of light and heavy cream for the milk and serve with toast points.

Oyster Fritters
Also known as Cutlets or Dodgers

    2½ dozen half-shell oysters, shucked
    2 cups sifted flour
    1 Tbsp baking powder
    1 tsp celery salt
    pinch of nutmeg
    1 Tbsp minced onion
    1 Tbsp finely chopped parsley
    ⅛ tsp white pepper
    2 eggs, beaten
    ½ cup milk
    ½ cup oyster liquor
    1 Tbsp melted butter
    fat or oil for frying

Method—Drain oysters, reserve liquor, and chop small. Sift dry ingredients together. Combine beaten eggs, milk, oyster liquor, and butter. Pour dry ingredients into liquid and stir until smooth; add chopped oysters. Drop batter by the teaspoonful into hot fat, heated to 350°, and fry 3 minutes or until golden brown. Drain on absorbent paper.

Yield: 6 servings

Salsify or Oyster Plant

Salsify is a vegetable and member of the sunflower family. Originating in the Mediterranean area, this plant was well known to the Romans and Greeks. Because its slightly metallic taste and soft texture resembles that of the delicious bivalve, the plant is frequently called the oyster plant or vegetable oyster. The oyster plant is rich in phosphorus, iron, and calcium, but does not provide large amounts of vitamins.

The roots of this plant are best eaten shortly after being dug up, as the oyster taste rapidly decreases with storage. The oyster plant may be boiled, fried, baked, sauteed, or served in soup and, in general, may be prepared in the same manner as parsnips. It is best prepared by steaming or cooking the unpeeled, raw root in slightly acidic water, (to prevent the root from turning brown) for approximately 20 minutes, or until tender. The raw plant is common in Europe but is marketed mostly in cans in the United States.

Sauteed Oyster Plant

  2 oz butter
  2 lb oyster plant (approximately 16 to 18 roots)
  1½ oz shallots
  ¼ tsp celery salt
  pinch parsley

Method—Cook oyster plant until tender, and peel. Cut into half-inch pieces. Saute shallots in butter, toss in oyster plant and celery salt. Saute lightly; sprinkle with parsley.

Yield: 6 to 8 portions

Cocktail Sauce

  ½ pt chili sauce
  ¼ cup tomato catsup
  2 oz prepared horseradish
  1 Tbsp lemon juice
  ¼ tsp Worcestershire sauce

Method—Combine all ingredients and chill. If a stronger sauce is desired, more horseradish and hot sauce may be added.

Yield: Approximately ½ quart

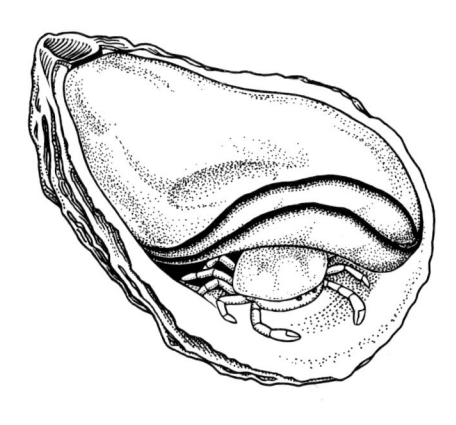

Oyster Crabs

The little oyster crab (Pinnotheres ostreum) is familiar to all connoisseurs of fresh oysters and has long been famous as a costly, choise morsel much sought after by gourmets. They are peculiar to only certain oysters, particularly those from the Chesapeake waters, but are seldom found in great abundance. The tiny crabs are about the size of a man's fingernail, with soft shells, smooth, shiny body surfaces, and rudimentary claws. The female crab takes shelter within the shell and lives in harmony with the oyster in the same compartment. The male crab has a thicker shell and, so far as is known, is a free-swimmer and for these reasons is of no significant economic or gastronomic importance.

In shucking houses and restaurants, where large numbers of oysters are constantly being opened, the crabs are saved but the difficulty of collecting together so many small creatures renders them very expensive; fewer than thirty crabs may be found in a barrel of oysters. They are then sold either fresh or pickled in jars in the larger cities, such as New York, to wealthy gourmets.

The crabs are frequently eaten alive and crawling along with the oyster with which they are associated as a messmate. Their flavor is sweet and delicate and they are very rich; one pound of them is a sufficient serving for four people. Oyster crabs are also served as garnishes with seafood or dusted with flour and fried with whitebait as an entree.

Oyster Crabs Newburg

Wash and drain the oyster crabs; fry them in butter; season with salt and cayenne pepper; toss them well and moisten with a little sherry wine and a little cream. Let cook for a minute before serving; thicken with egg yolks diluted with cream and a little brandy; add a piece of fresh butter; stir on the fire without boiling. Serve in a chafing dish.

Oysters on the Half-Shell

6 half-shell or medium oysters per person

2 oz cocktail sauce per person

1 lemon wedge

parsley sprig for garnish

crushed ice

Method — Chill oysters. Open the shell oysters utilizing one of the techniques described in the chapter on Serving. Place the meat on either the flat or deep half of the shell, as desired. Arrange the oysters on the oyster plate, or like spokes on a wheel in shallow bowls or soup plates with shaved or cracked ice. Place the container of cocktail sauce in the middle and garnish with parsley and lemon wedge. Appropriate condiments include — vinegar, fresh ground pepper, Worcestershire sauce, Tabasco, oyster crackers, horseradish, brown or French bread and butter.

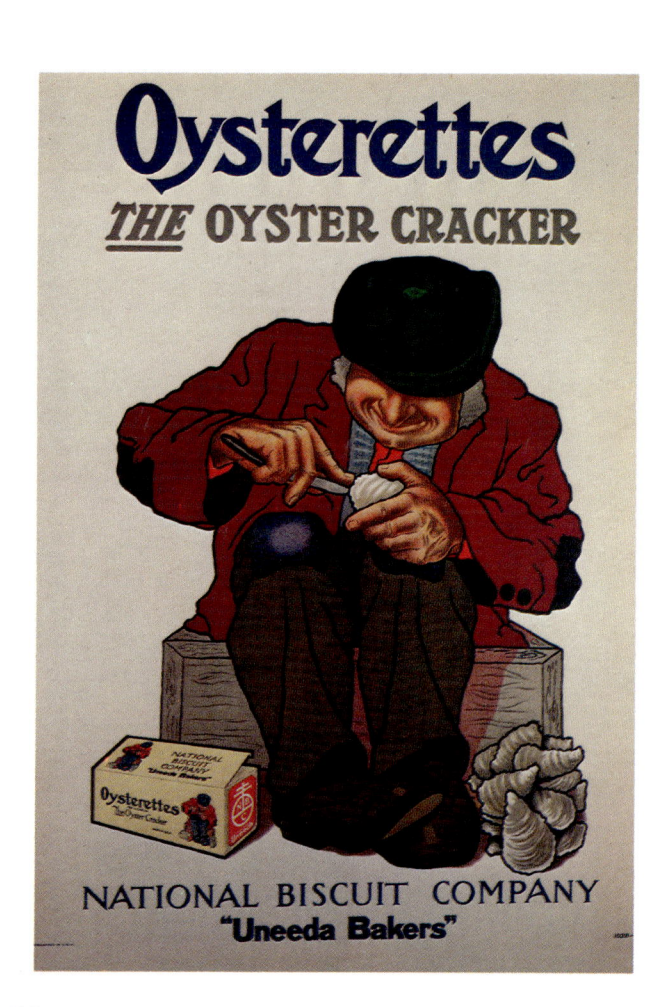

Courtesy of The Old Print Shop, Kenneth M. Newman

No dish or bowl of oyster stew is complete without an accompaniment of crackers and, in many cases, the oyster cracker is a standard table condiment in seafood and oyster houses. In the 19th century, there were many cracker companies, including one patented brand, Hartman's, which were shaped in the form of an oyster. With the decline of the popularity of oysters in the early 1900's, many of these firms ceased production.

One of the earliest and best known of the oyster cracker manufacturers was established in 1848 in New Jersey. Today, the Original Trenton Cracker Company and the O-T-C oyster cracker are world famous. These crackers are baked by an exclusive triple heat process which has been perfected and maintained by four generations of family ownership and attention. These crackers are full-bodied, even-textured and have a special, baked crispness that make a perfect combination with an oyster stew. They are made from natural ingredients including polyunsaturated shortening and these flavorful crackers come packaged in familiar yellow bags labeled O-T-C.

Other companies which prepare oyster crackers include Nabisco, which makes a delightfully thin cracker called an Oysterette in small packages and Dandy in larger boxes. Oyster and soup crackers are also manufactured by the Sunshine Company and can be easily found on supermarket shelves. Both crackers are excellent for snacks or for use with soup.

HISTORY OF THE OYSTER MUSEUM OF CHINCOTEAGUE

In 1965, while discussing a means to preserve the culture and heritage of the island, a group of Chincoteague ladies gave birth to an idea. This idea would become the Oyster Museum of Chincoteague.

After much hard work, and a real love for the project, the museum was finally opened to the public in 1972. The museum itself is unique as it is the only one of its kind in the United States. It tells the story of the seafood business, and mainly focuses on the oyster because it is the major industry of the island.

The museum also shows live exhibits of the animals that are found in the channel waters. There are all the implements used in farming the oyster; with many turn-of-the-century methods. A diorama that shows the channel area, complete with scows, monitors, and the shucking process, is a must for all visitors to the museum.

The Maddox library is complete with books and papers for the most ambitious student of marine life. Films are also shown from time to time.

Hopefully, the museum will continue to grow with the years. New additions are made continuously, and that gives fresh insight on the beautiful island of Chincoteague, Virginia.

Chincoteague Oyster Souffle

    2 cans (10 oz each) oysters, fresh or frozen
    ½ cup chopped onion
    ⅓ cup margarine or butter
    ½ cup flour
    1½ tsp salt
    ½ tsp paprika
    dash pepper
    dash nutmeg
    1 cup milk
    4 eggs, separated

Method — Thaw oysters; drain and reserve ½ cup liquor. Coarsely chop oysters. Cook onion slowly in saucepan in butter or margarine until tender, not brown. Stir in flour, salt, pepper, paprika, and nutmeg. Add milk and reserve oyster liquor; cook until thickened, stirring constantly. Remove from heat. Beat egg yolks until thick and lemony colored. Add egg yolks to hot mixture slowly, stirring constantly. Fold in oysters. Beat egg whites until they hold soft peaks. Carefully fold whites into oyster mixture. Pour into ungreased two-quart deep casserole. Bake in slow oven — 325° — for 65 minutes, or until souffle is puffed, brown and set. Serve with creamy lemon sauce.

Yield: 6 servings

Creamy Lemon Sauce

    2 Tbsp margarine or butter
    2 Tbsp flour
    ½ tsp salt
    ¼ tsp paprika
    1¼ cup milk
    ½ cup mayonnaise
    1 Tbsp lemon juice

Method — Melt butter in saucepan. Stir in flour, salt, and paprika. Add milk; cook until thickened and smooth, stirring constantly. Blend in mayonnaise and lemon juice; heat. Serve over oyster souffle.

A "RARE-BIT"

Oyster Rarebit

    24 small oysters, drained
    1 oz butter
    8 oz Cooper cheese, grated
    ¼ cup oyster liquor
    ¼ tsp celery salt
    pinch cayenne pepper
    2 eggs
    ¼ cup heavy cream

Method — Drain oysters, reserving the liquor, and add cream and slightly beaten eggs. Using a heavy bottomed pan and medium heat, melt butter; add cheese and seasonings. As cheese melts, add oyster liquor, eggs and cream gradually. When the mixture is smooth, add the oysters. (Oyster meat may also be mashed and then incorporated into the cheese mixture.) Serve on bread that has been toasted on one side. Pour or ladle rarebit over the untoasted side.

Yield: 3 to 4 portions

S.S. KEELING & CO.
WHOLESALE PACKERS & PLANTERS
LITTLE BAY OYSTERS

We ship the finest Brands of Oysters open and in Shell that can be gotten in Tidewater, Va. to all Parts of the United States.

OYSTER'S TWO

"How dreadfully hot it is."
"Yes. I feel quite in a stew."

Thomas Jefferson's Creamed Oysters and Eggs

1 pt. fresh shucked select Virginia Oysters
1 tablespoon margarine or butter
1 tablespoon all-purpose flour
½ teaspoon salt
1 can (10-¾ oz.) condensed cream of celery soup
½ cup evaporated milk
2 hard cooked eggs, sliced
1 can (2 oz.) mushroom stems and pieces, drained
2 tablespoons chopped pimentoes
2 tablespoons chopped parsley
4 large baking powder biscuits* or patty shells

Remove any remaining particles of shell. In a 2 quart saucepan, melt margarine. Add oysters and oyster liquor and cook slowly until edges curl, stirring constantly. Stir in flour and salt. Add soup and milk; cook stirring constantly until sauce is smooth and hot. Add eggs, mushrooms, pimento and parsley; stir gently until well mixed and heat. Spoon over hot biscuits or into patty shells. Serves 4.

*Using 2 cups of prepared biscuit mix or self-rising flour, prepare and bake large biscuits as directed on package label.

Scalloped Oysters with Pecans

1 pt. fresh shucked standard Virginia Oysters
¾ cup melted butter or margarine, divided
1 teaspoon finely grated onion
¼ teaspoon each salt, fresh ground pepper and crumbled thyme
3 cups fine soft bread crumbs, preferably from French style sourdough
½ cup finely chopped pecans
parsley sprigs for garnish (optional)

Drain oysters and remove any remaining shell particles. Pat dry. Dip oysters in butter to coat; arrange in single layer in baking dish. Sprinkle with onion, salt, pepper and thyme. Toss bread crumbs with all except 2 tablespoons remaining butter; sprinkle over oysters. Bake in preheated 350° oven 20 to 25 minutes until oysters are done. If desired, place under broiler to brown crumbs. Meanwhile sauté pecans in reserved 2 tablespoons butter until lightly toasted; sprinkle over crumbs. Garnish with parsley. Makes 4 servings.

Old-Fashioned Oyster Chowder

1 pint oysters, fresh or frozen, undrained
8 strips bacon, diced
2 T. butter or margarine
2 cups cooked potatoes, coarsely chopped
½ cup sliced green onion or 1 medium onion, chopped
½ cup diced celery
1 medium carrot, coarsely shredded
½ cup water
2 cups milk
2 cups half and half
1 can (12 oz.) whole kernel corn, drained
1½ t. salt
⅛ t. white pepper
2 dashes liquid hot pepper sauce
chopped parsley

Thaw oysters if frozen. Fry bacon over moderate heat in large Dutch oven until crisp. Remove bacon, reserve. Remove all but 2 tablespoons of bacon drippings from pan; add margarine or butter. Sauté potatoes in drippings until lightly browned. Add onions, celery, carrots, and water; cover and simmer about 5 minutes or until vegetables are tender. Add milk, half and half, corn, salt, pepper and liquid hot pepper sauce. Simmer. Add oysters, oyster liquid, and bacon. Heat just until edges of oysters curl. Add liquid hot pepper sauce. Ladle into soup bowls; sprinkle with parsley. Makes about 10 cups, 6 to 8 servings.

Recipes Developed by The Virginia Seafood Council

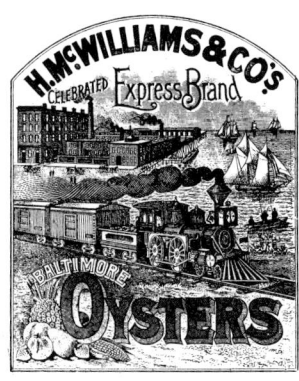

Oysters Chancery

1 teaspoon chicken seasoned stock base (or chicken bouillon cube)
1 cup boiling water
¼ cup (½ stick) margarine or butter
3 tablespoons flour
¼ cup Smithfield ham, coarsely chopped
1 jar (⅝-ounce) freeze-dried mushroom slices, reconstituted or 1 2-ounce can mushrooms with liquid)
1 heaping teaspoon freeze-dried chopped chives
1 tablespoon soy sauce
1 teaspoon instant minced onion
½ teaspoon lemon and pepper seasoning
⅛ teaspoon garlic powder
1 pint shucked Maryland standard oysters, with liquor
2 tablespoons margarine or butter
8 patty shells
Paprika, for garnish

Dissolve chicken stock base in boiling water. In 2-quart pan, melt margarine or butter, stir in flour. Slowly add chicken liquid, stirring constantly, to keep mixture smooth and free from lumps. Cook, stirring, over medium heat until mixture comes to a boil and thickens. Reduce heat, add ham, mushrooms with liquid and seasonings to sauce. Simmer, stirring, 2 to 3 minutes to blend flavors.

In another pan, simmer oysters, with liquor, in margarine or butter until edges of oysters just begin to curl. Using slotted spoon, add oysters to sauce. Use oyster liquid, if needed, to thin sauce to desired consistency.

When ready to serve, fill patty shells with oyster mixture. Sprinkle paprika over top of each filled shell. Place on cookie sheet and broil, 4 inches from source of heat, until hot and bubbly, 1 to 2 minutes. Serve immediately.

Serve 1 patty shell per person as a first course; 2 per person as a main course.

NOTE: 36 petite patty shells may be used and served as hot appetizers.

*Recipes Developed by
The Maryland Seafood Marketing Authority*

Old Line Oyster Pie

Pastry for double crust 9-inch pie
2 cups thinly sliced potatoes, slightly undercooked
1 pint shucked Maryland oysters, with liquor
4 hard cooked eggs, shelled and sliced
¼ cup margarine or butter (½ stick)
Celery salt, to taste
Lemon and pepper seasoning, to taste

Place bottom crust in pie pan. Put in well-drained potatoes. Remove oysters from container with slotted spoon and put over potatoes (reserve oyster liquid for sauce). Place egg slices over oysters. Dot margarine or butter over top and sprinkle with celery salt and lemon and pepper seasoning. Place top crust on pie. Cut slits in top to allow steam to escape.

Bake at 400°F for 10 minutes; lower heat and bake at 375°F, until crust is lightly browned, about 30 minutes. Let stand a few minutes before serving (drain off any excess liquid). Serve with oyster sauce.

Makes 6 servings.

Oyster Sauce (for pie)

2 tablespoons margarine or butter
2 tablespoons flour
1 cup milk
Oyster liquid plus water to equal ½ cup
Salt, to taste
Pepper, to taste

In medium-size pan, melt margarine or butter, mix in flour. Slowly add milk, then oyster liquor, stirring constantly, to keep mixture smooth and free from lumps. Cook, stirring, over medium heat until mixture comes to a boil and thickens. Add salt and pepper.

Serve hot with pie.

National Oyster Cook-Off

The St. Mary's County Oyster Cook-Off, a spin-off of the annual Oyster Festival in Leonardtown, Maryland, has grown into The National Oyster Cook-Off. In October, people from all across the nation vie for the top price of $625.00 and the honor of the first place award.

Deep South Cornbread Dressing with Oysters
First Prize Winner, National Oyster Cook-Off
Patricia D. Russell, Lexington Park, Md.

Egg Bread —
- 4 eggs
- 2½ cups yellow cornbread
- 2 cups buttermilk
- 3 Tbsp melted shortening
- 2 tsp salt
- 1 tsp soda
- 3 tsp baking powder

Dressing —
- 1 recipe egg bread
- 2 cups dry white bread cubes
- ½ cup butter
- ⅓ cup chopped onion
- ½ cup chopped celery
- ¼ cup fresh parsley
- 1 tsp salt
- ¼ tsp pepper
- 1 tsp poultry seasoning or sage
- 1 pint oysters
- 2 cups chicken broth

Method — Make egg bread the day before you intend to serve the dressing. Beat eggs until light, add milk, shortening, and salt. Mix, add baking powder and soda. Mix thoroughly, add cornmeal; beat until smooth by hand. Bake in a greased one quart bread pan at 400° until top is golden brown. Cool, remove from pan and crumble.

When ready to make dressing, melt butter in a skillet. Brown onion and celery. Chop oysters. In a large bowl, combine the crumbled egg bread, the browned onion and celery and all remaining ingredients. Stir and fold until all ingredients are thoroughly mixed and moistened.

19th Century can label

This dressing may be used to stuff poultry or as a side dish by baking in a greased casserole dish at 350° for 20 to 30 minutes.

Oyster Stuffing
First Prize Winner, National Oyster Cook-Off
Lynda Wernsing, Riviera Beach, Md.

- 16 oz oysters, drained and coarsely chopped
- 5 cups bread cubes
- 4 eggs, hard-boiled and chopped
- ¼ cup butter or margarine
- ½ cup chopped onion
- ½ cup chopped celery
- ¼ tsp Old Bay Seasoning or pepper
- ½ tsp garlic powder (optional)
- ½ cup chicken broth, or ½ cup water with one chicken boullion cube

Method — Sauté onions and celery in butter about 5 minutes. In large bowl, gently mix bread cubes, oysters and eggs. Stir the seasonings and broth into onion and celery; bring to a boil. Pour liquid mixture over dry ingredients and toss until moistened. Place in a 1½ quart baking dish. Bake uncovered in 350° oven 25 to 30 minutes or until heated throughout.

If a chicken stuffing is desired, allow about one cup of stuffing per each pound of chicken.

Or, if microwave oven is used, cook about 15 minutes, uncovered, turning dish ¼ turn every 4 minutes.

Tidewater Stew
Second Prize Winner National Oyster Cook-Off
Anita M. Meridith, Mechanicsville, Md.

- 1 quart oysters
- 3 cups diced boiled potatoes
- 1 cup finely chopped onion
- 1 cup finely chopped celery
- ¼ cup fried, crumbled bacon
- 2 sticks butter
- 1 cup slivered mushrooms
- ¼ cup finely chopped green pepper
- dash of salt, black pepper, red pepper and oregano
- 4 cups whole milk

Method — In saucepan, saute butter, onion, celery, green pepper and mushrooms. Put in large kettle and add oysters, milk, and potatoes. Bring to simmer and add sautéed ingredients. When oysters have curled in the stew, add crumbled bacon and sprinkle on oregano. Serve hot with generous serving of buttered cornbread.

UNION OYSTER HOUSE
Since 1826

A Boston Tradition
41 UNION STREET, BOSTON — 227-2750

Heritage of Ye Olde Oyster House

The Union Oyster House is the oldest restaurant in Boston and the oldest restaurant in continuous service in the U.S.—the doors have always been open to diners since 1826.

Union Street was laid out in 1636, but there are no municipal records documenting the Oyster House's date of construction. All that is known is that the building has stood on Union Street as a major local landmark for more than 250 years.

In 1742—before it became a seafood house—the building housed importer Hopestill Capen's fancy dress goods business, known colorfully as "At the Sign of the Cornfields."

The first stirrings of the American Revolution reached the upper floor of the building in 1771 when printer Isaiah Thomas published his newspaper "The Massachusetts Spy," long known as the oldest newspaper in the United States.

In 1775 Capen's Silk and Dry Goods Store became headquarters for Ebenezer Hancock, the first paymaster of the Continental Army. There is no reason to doubt that Washington himself was familiar with its surroundings. At the very spot where diners today enjoy their favorite New England specialties, Federal troops received their "war wages" in the official pay-station.

In 1796, a future king of France lived on the second floor. Exiled from his country, he earned his living by teaching French to many of Boston's fashionable young ladies. Later Louis Philippe returned home to serve as King from 1830 to 1848.

1826 marked the end of Capen's Dry Goods Store and the beginning of Atwood and Bacon's establishment. The new owners installed the fabled Semi-Circular Oyster Bar—where the greats of Boston paused for refreshment.

It was at the Oyster Bar that Daniel Webster, a constant customer, daily drank his tall tumbler of brandy and water with each half-dozen oysters, seldom having less than 6 plates.

The oldest oyster shucker in the U.S., Thomas Butt, now in his eighties, can still be seen practicing his art every day behind the world famous oyster bar.

The Toothpick was first used in the U.S. at Union Oyster House. Enterprising Charles Forster of Maine first imported the picks from South America. To promote his new business, he hired Harvard boys to dine at the Oyster House and ask for toothpicks.

A college president was salad man here. Jack Coleman, President of Pennsylvania's Haverford College, worked in total anonymity for a few months during his sabbatical when he secretly sampled some of America's rigorous jobs and lifestyles.

The Kennedy Clan has patronized the Union Oyster House for years. J.F.K. loved to feast in privacy in the upstairs dining room. His favorite booth "The Kennedy Booth" has since been dedicated in his memory.

The Union Oyster House has known only three owners since 1826. Today the Milano family carries on the proud tradition in fine dining.

Oysters Primavera

    24 shucked oysters
    3 oz butter
    2 oz minced carrot
    2 oz minced onion
    4 oz minced zuccini
    2 oz minced pimento
    3 oz flour
    16 oz half and half
    4 oz grated cheese
    salt and pepper to taste (or garlic powder)

Method—Saute minced vegetables in butter in 2 qt sauce pot to tender. Add flour and cook for 2-3 minutes. Add half and half. Mix until thick 5-10 minutes. Finish with cheese and salt and pepper.

Let mixture cool, then stuff the oysters and bake for 15 minutes at 325°.

Union Stuffed Oysters

    24 oysters in half shell
    2 oz oil (olive)
    2 oz garlic
    4 oz chopped mushrooms
    4 ox I.Q.F. baby shrimp
    8 oz spinach chopped cooked
    2 whole eggs
    4- 6 oz bread crumbs
        (options: ritz crackers and potato chips)

Method—In sauté pan heat oil and sauté garlic to color change then add mushroom. Cook to tender. Add shrimp and spinach and cook until shrimp is done. Remove from heat and allow to cool 5 minutes. To this pan add crumbs, eggs, and seasoning. When mixture is cool, oysters can be stuffed. Bake 15 minutes at 325°.

Bought of **ATWOOD & BACON,** *Wholesale and Retail Dealers in* **OYSTERS**

Felix's Restaurant, Inc.

739 IBERVILLE STREET
NEW ORLEANS, LOUISIANA 70130

Famous for Oysters

Located just a few steps off Bourbon Street (and just about as well-known) is an oyster bar that's a favorite of locals and visitors from coast to coast. Felix's Restaurant and Oyster Bar has been shucking oysters and serving delectable seafood to its loyal following for over four decades. Businessmen arriving in New Orleans are ever known to ask their cab driver to take them directly to Felix's for a dozen salty ones before going to the hotel. Of course, some people we know, who don't even like oysters, will stop off at Felix's just to watch the master shuckers at work. It's great entertainment and there's no cover charge!

Although Felix's is nationally known for its oyster and raw bar, it also prepares oysters more than a dozen different ways, has a complete line of fresh seafood available and offers seafood dishes to please even the most discriminating palates.

The two dining rooms at Felix's are decorated attractively in a nautical motif with lots of artwork on the walls depicting regional fishing scenes.

Mr. Lemon—"Can I do anything for you Miss Shell?"
Miss Shell—"No thank you. I can get along without Lemon-aide."

Oyster and Spaghetti

    4 doz. shelled oysters
      (reserve and strain liquor)
    ½ cup olive oil
    ½ cup chopped shallots (green onion)
    4 cloves garlic, minced
    ¼ cup chopped parsley
    Grated Parmesan Cheese
    1 lb. cooked spaghetti
    Salt & pepper (cayenne) to taste

Method—Sauté shallots, garlic, parsley in heated olive oil until wilted. Poach oysters in their own liquor until edges curl. Add oysters and strained hot liquid to the oil and cooked seasoning allowing to cook an additional 2 or 3 minutes. Pour over hot spaghetti and top with grated cheese.

Oyster Brochette

    2 doz. raw oysters
    14 slices bacon
    1 cup flour
    1 tablespoon cayenne
    1 cup egg wash
    4 metal skewers

Method—Skewer oyster between half slice of bacon such that bacon is folded in W or N shape with oyster between bacon strips. (6 oysters to a skewer). Dip skewer in egg wash and dust with flour mixed with cayenne. Deep fry in hot cooking oil until done.

Serve with lemon wedge and garnish with parsley.

OVER 100 YEARS OF FINE FOOD
Since 1867

Maye's OYSTER HOUSE

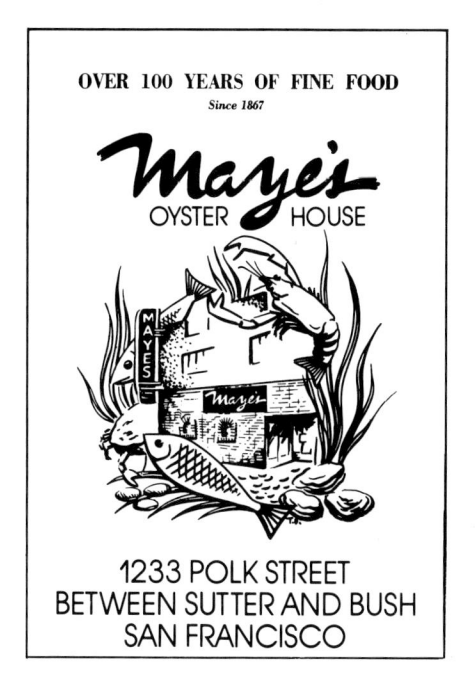

1233 POLK STREET
BETWEEN SUTTER AND BUSH
SAN FRANCISCO

Maye's Oyster House

Maye's Oyster House has been the favorite of politicians, cops, firemen, and the beau monde since it first opened in the California Market, an outdoor wholesale produce area, in 1867. Sometime in the 1880's, the Yugoslavian family who ran the establishment divided it into two restaurants, leaving one in the California Market, moving the other to Polk Street.

During his long tenure in City Hall, Mayor "Sunny" Jim Rolph, who genially presided over San Francisco during the golden years of 1911 to 1930, would often end a long day at the counter of Maye's over oyster loaf and clam chowder, or begin the morning's labors with one of his favorite breakfasts, boiled turbot. San Francisco novelist Gertrude Atherton (1857-1948) was another habitue of Maye's, linking this rather unpretentious establishment with the world of society. Mrs. Atherton loved the breaded Olympia oysters. Jack London relished Maye's Hangtown fries.

Maye's is an established San Francisco tradition serving excellent seafood at inexpensive prices. Their delicious seafood dinners, complete with soup, salad, seafood cocktail, pasta and dessert, could be the best deal in town! The oyster of course, is presented in every imaginable manner.

Oysters Kirkpatrick

2 dozen half-shell oysters
12 bacon strips
1 cup ketchup
1 tsp Worcestershire sauce
dash hot sauce
chopped parsley, lemon wedge

Method—Mix ketchup, Worcestershire sauce and hot sauce. Set oysters in bottom half of deep shells. Spoon sauce over tops and place one half bacon strip over. Bake at 400° for 5 to 7 minutes. Sprinkle with chopped parsley and serve with lemon wedge.

Yield: 4 portions

Hangtown Fry

A legendary concoction with a colorful, though uncertain, history. Most authorities agree that the fish was first served in California during the Gold Rush days of the mid 1800's. As the story goes, a successful miner with a hungry appetite and pockets laden with gold nuggets, instructed a Hangtown cook to prepare him the finest, most expensive meal. At the time, all provisions were costly, but oysters and eggs were the most expensive items on the menu. The cook combined the two and served them up, thus creating a memorable dish whose fame spread over the surrounding areas, including San Francisco. It soon became fashionable for gentlemen of the day to order a few drinks and a Hangtown Fry.

5 half-shell oysters, shucked
2 strips bacon
2 or 3 eggs, per serving
1 tsp cold water
celery salt to taste
white pepper or hot sauce to taste
clarified butter

Method—Either par-boil or dip oysters in cracker meal and fry lightly. Beat eggs; add water and season to taste. Par-cook bacon and chop into small pieces. Heat butter; pour in egg mixture and as egg sets, add oysters and bacon; fold over and finish in oven. Serve with homefries and garnish with parsley.

NOTE: Oysters may be cut into smaller pieces and added to egg mixture along with bacon prior to pouring into pan, if desired.

Yield: 1 serving

ALARMING PROPOSITION.
Oyster Man (to Hairy Gents). "Oysters, sir! Yes, sir! Shall I take yer beards off?" *(Gents have an uncomfortable idea that they are being chaffed.)*
by John Leach, 1866

*Three Generations of Fine Dining.**

This is our story!

Atlantic City, 1897. It was a growth year. The rich and the not-so-rich flocked to the fabled sands of Atlantic City to breathe the clean salt air, patronize the posh hotels that lined the oceanfront, escape the hot and humid air of Philadelphia, Camden, New York and countless other towns, large and small, that dotted the East. It was a good year in which a fine dinner might cost you as much as 75¢! Shrimp was 15¢ a pound by the barrel. The two-piece bathing suit was appearing to shock the Mainline matrons along the shore!

This was an important year for another reason, too. It was in 1897 that young Harry Dougherty tacked up his sign over the about-to-open *"Dock's Oyster House"*. Harry ("call me Dock") believed there was a need for a seafood house that would prepare the finest seafood, as carefully as possible, and serve it in the cleanest and friendliest of surroundings. He was right.

The depressions across the years came and went and Harry, because of his uncompromising standards, economically survived. And, so did Dock's!

When Harry's health declined in 1938 his son, Joseph the second generation, assumed ownership of the restaurant. A few years later came World War II and Joseph was called to duty. However, with the able management of his wife, Anne, the restaurant continued and blossomed. When Joseph returned in 1945, he enlarged the restaurant to 80 seats.

It was in 1969, upon the retirement of Joseph, Sr., that Harry's grandson, Joseph, Jr., the third generation, took the next daring step. The decline and decay of cities all over the country has not spared Atlantic City. The dowager Queen of Resorts was fading. But, Joe, Jr., still believed in the old "Queen" and felt that if the business people in Atlantic City would refurbish, the city would

2405 Atlantic Ave.
Atlantic City, New Jersey

once again prosper! With this philosophy, and a good deal of courage, he proceeded to completely renovate *"Docks"*. The entire building was gutted to house two completely modern kitchens, a 120-seat dining room in a nautical decor and—something *Dock's* never had—a small service bar that served alcoholic beverages.

The next decade was a rough one . . . seafood prices skyrocketed, convention business had almost disappeared, city morale was at its lowest ebb.

Joe, Jr., decided to work the "back of the house". He did most of the cooking himself, cleaned and boned all of the fresh fish that he ordered, and did the baking! He asked his wife, Arleen, to join him and see to the comfort and satisfaction of his guests in the dining room. His sons, Joe III and Frank, then very young boys, also pitched in and did all kinds of chores to help their Dad.

So, with the aid of his family, and his loyal crew, Joe, Jr., preserved and saw his dream for the rebirth of his city and the continued success of his restaurant, come true!

In 1979, in keeping with the revitalization of Atlantic City through the advent of casino gambling, Joe, Jr., decided to once again refurbish the dining room and add a small, intimate cocktail lounge.

With the assistance of a very talented architect, Stanford G. Brooks; a very imaginative designer, Raymond C. Perko, and a very cooperative local contractor, Jack Dillon, we were able to create an exciting new feeling without changing the friendly, relaxed atmosphere that has always been *Dock's*.

Today, Joe, Jr., is still "in the kitchen"; wife Arleen is in the dining room and, on weekends, Joe III is at the register while son Frank is cooking with his Dad. Other family members, employees that have been seen for more than three decades at Dock's, as well as newcomers, complete our friendly staff. And, we're all here to please you!

A PERSONAL NOTE...

We are excited about our "new" city as well as our "new/old" restaurant—and would like to share this feeling with you.

Although we are pleased with our new ambience, we will never lose sight of the fact that enjoyment of your dinner is our prime consideration—and we pledge to you that we will continue to maintain the highest standards of quality excellence initiated by our Grandfather Harry, over eight long decades ago!

We invite you to relax and enjoy your visit. Come back real soon! It's our pleasure to serve you.

Your hosts, Arleen & Joe

Barbecued Oysters

Use Florida Peanut Oysters. Grill 1 doz. oysters cup side down, so that they cook in their own juice. Do not turn oysters during cooking. They are done when the shells pop open, about 8 minutes. Serve the oysters on the half-shell with lemon garlic butter.

Hot Lemon Garlic Butter

1 small clove garlic—chopped or pressed
Juice of half a lemon
2 oz of butter

Serves four

Courtesy Mr. Frank Cagianese

Courtesy Dave Mink, Sansom St. Oyster House

Sansom St. Oyster House

Sansom St., Philadelphia, Pa.

Sansom Street Oyster Pan Roast

    1 shallot
    4 sprigs parsley, chopped
    1 Tbsp margarine
    1 Tbsp flour
    1 cup water
    salt and pepper
    1 dozen oysters
    bread crumbs

Method — Boil oysters in one cup of water until edges curl, and drain, reserving liquid. Sauté shallots and parsley in margarine; stir in flour and blend in water from oysters, slowly to make a thick sauce. Season to taste. Put six oysters in each individual casserole dish or ramekin and cover with sauce. Sprinkle with bread crumbs. Bake about 15 minutes at 350°.

Yield: 2 servings

The Sansom St. Oyster House, founded May, 1976, traces its roots back to 1947. That was the year that the owner's father, Samuel Mink, gave up his law practice for a career in the restaurant business. Mink purchased Kelly's on Mole Street from the Kelly Estate. Kelly's stayed at that location from 1901 to 1969 when it was forced to move because of urban renewal. Mink died before the new restaurant opened; however, his son David and daughter Nancy saw to it that the new restaurant continued operating.

Kelly's on Mole Street is now closed; but the tradition of fresh seafood, simply prepared at reasonable prices, lives on at the Sansom Street Oyster House.

The restaurant has the same charm and friendliness that Kelly's, the local oyster bar, did at the turn of the century. The Oyster House features the largest collection of antique oyster plates in Philadelphia. It is a collection that has been fifty years in the making. As in the beginning, the Sansom Street Oyster House still hosts many of Philadelphia's lawyers and judges at lunch and the local residents for dinner.

Grand Central Station
New York City

Opened in 1913, The Grand Central Oyster Bar Restaurant, located in Grand Central Terminal, New York City, is famous for its elegant beaux-arts architectural design as well as for its great seafood.

Serving as many as two thousand people a day, the "Oyster Bar" presents an unequaled variety of the world's finest fresh seafood prepared to perfection by Master Chefs.

Oyster Stew (Individual)

    8 freshly opened oysters with oyster liquor
    2 Tbsp (¼ stick) butter
    dash celery salt
    2 Tbsp clam juice
    1 tsp Worcestershire sauce
    ½ tsp paprika
    1 cup half and half

Method—Place all ingredients, except half and half and 1 Tbsp of butter in top part of double boiler over boiling water. Don't let top pan touch water. Stir briskly for one minute, or until edges of oysters curl. Add half and half and stir to boil. *Do not boil!* Pour into oyster stew bowl; add remaining butter and sprinkle with paprika.

Oyster Pan Roast (Individual)

    8 freshly opened oysters with oyster liquor
    2 Tbsp (¼ stick) butter
    1 Tbsp chili sauce
    1 tsp Worcestershire sauce
    2 Tbsp clam juice
    ½ tsp paprika
    dash of celery salt
    1 cup half and half
    1 slice dry toast

Method—Place all ingredients except half and half, toast and one tablespoon of butter in top part of double boiler over boiling water. (Don't let top pan touch water.) Stir for one minute, or until edges of oysters curl. Add half and half; bring to boil, but do not boil. Pour Pan Roast into soup plate over dry toast. Top with remaining butter and sprinkle with paprika. Serve.

Blanquette de Belons aux Poireaux

    5 freshly opened Belon oysters on the half shell
    1 Tbsp leeks, cut in 1½" julienne
    1 tsp chopped shallots
    1 tsp butter
    2 Tbsp white wine
    6 oz heavy cream
    salt and pepper

Method—Saute chopped shallots in butter until soft. Add heavy cream and reduce by ⅓. Warm oysters in their juice and white wine until edges curl. Add wine and juice from oysters to the cream and reduce by half. Meanwhile, cover oysters and keep warm. Add previously blanched leeks to sauce. Check seasoning and reduce until sauce-like consistency.

To blanch leeks—Bring salted water to rapid boil. Put in leeks; cook 1 minute. Drain water; rinse with ice cold water to serve.

Put oysters in washed warm shells and coat with sauce. Serve on folded white napkins.

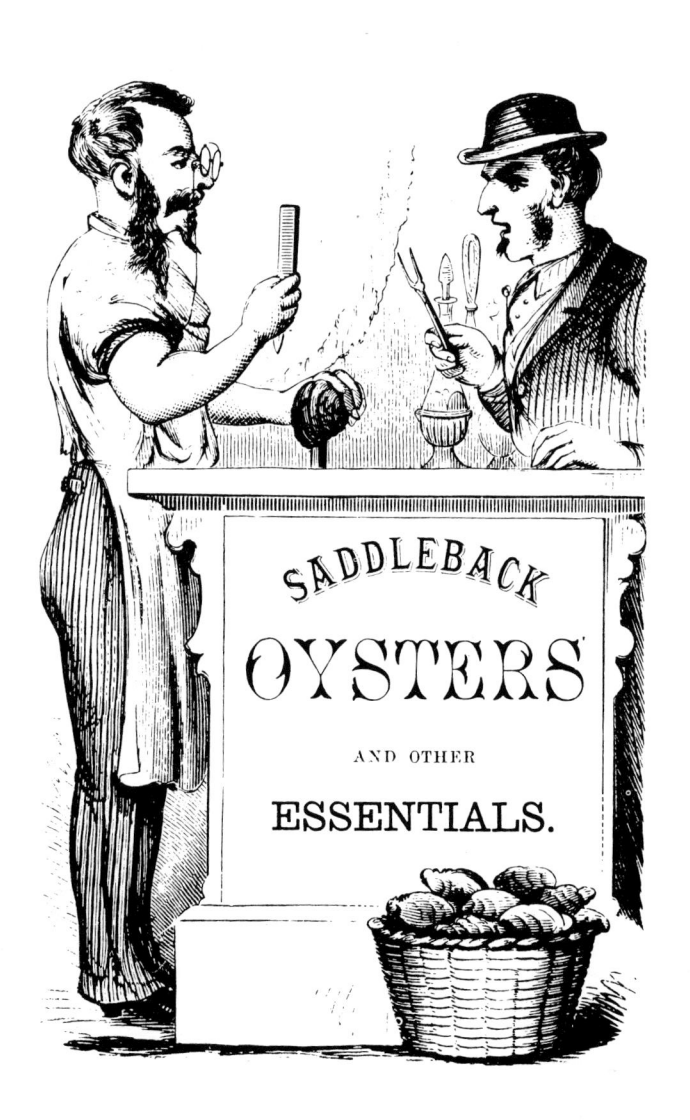

Gage & Tollner.

372 Fulton St.
Brooklyn, N.Y.

Interior of the Oyster and Chop House courtesy Mr. & Mrs. Dewey

History

1879 — Charles M. Gage founded an eating house at 302 Fulton Street in the heart of what was the birthplace of Brooklyn.

1884 — Eugene Tollner became associated with Charles M. Gage and the restaurant became known as Gage & Tollner.

1887 — The Statue of Liberty was unveiled and Gage and Tollner's fame spread as dignitaries from all over the country made the eating house their dining headquarters while in New York.

1889 — Gage and Tollner moved to its present location at 372 Fulton Street. The original decor, which was characteristic of the 1880's, has been preserved almost intact to this very day. It was a time when elegance in dining was beginning to play an important role in American life, fostered by Delmonico's and Rector's in Manhattan and, of course, Gage and Tollner in Brooklyn.

1911 — Messers. Gage and Tollner retired and sold the restaurant to two gentlemen by the names of Cunningham and Ingalls who agreed to maintain the policies of the founders.

1919 — Cunningham and Ingalls sold Gage & Tollner to Seth Bradford Dewey in association with his father, Hiram T. Dewey. Seth Bradford Dewey had conducted the restaurant of H.T. Dewey & Sons in Manhattan for 13 years. In addition to being part of a family long identified with restaurant ownership, Mr. Dewey had great experience in wine making. This heritage traced back to 1857, when Hiram T. Dewey planted the vineyards in the famous Catawba wine grape belt in the Lake Erie region of the United States.

1923 — The Dewey interests purchased the building housing Gage & Tollner, assuring its continuance at the same location and perpetuation as a prominent Brooklyn Landmark for an indefinite period.

1949 — Mr. Ed Dewey took over active management of Gage & Tollner, pledged to carry forward the policies and high quality standards of his predecessors.

1973 — Landmark hearings held with no demurrals. Mr. John B. Simmons joined with Ed Dewey in the ownership and management.

1974 — Exterior of Gage & Tollner officially designated as a Landmark.

1975 — Interior of Gage & Tollner officially designated as a Landmark.

Oysters Casino

12 oysters on the half shell
¼ cup finely chopped parsley
¼ cup finely chopped pimento
¼ cup finely chopped green pepper, blanched
¼ cup crisp bacon, crumbled
soft butter to bind.

Method — Mix all ingredients, except oysters, to form a loose paste. Spoon some of the mixture liberally on each oyster to cover it. Place oysters, in their shells, on a bed of rock salt on an oven-proof flat dish and put under a hot broiler, or in a hot oven for 5 minutes. Garnish with lemon wedges.

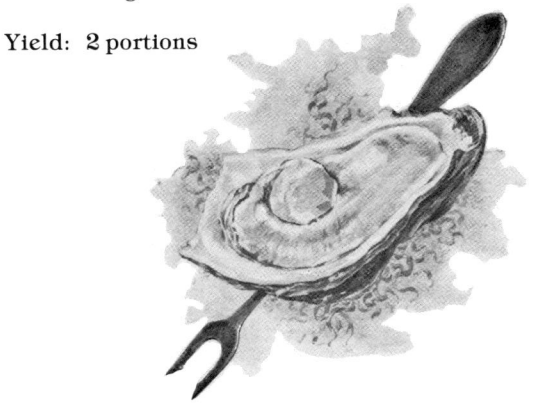

Yield: 2 portions

The Whistling Oyster

Ogunquit, Maine

In 1907, the Maine seacoast village of Ogunquit saw the birth of a pleasant tearoom and small gift shop overlooking the tranquil harbor at Perkins Cove, and catering to the carriage trade during the months of summer.

In the decades that followed, the establishment grew in size, expanded its service to include luncheon, dinner — even Sunday brunch — and earned an enviable reputation for both its incomparable Continental/American cuisine and distinctive gifts.

Today, The Whistling Oyster retains this reputation for excellence. Open year round, its location on the southern Maine coast makes it easily accessible all seasons. The emphasis is on leisurely dining in a warm, spacious interior of rich wood with colorful views capturing the quiet charm of the cove. Luncheon, dinner and cocktails are served daily; Sunday features the unique Champagne Brunch. There are also special facilities for private parties with a staff trained to plan and carry out every detail flawlessly.

The Gift Shop is filled with an uncommonly fine selection of jewelry, crystal, leather goods, accessories and cards.

The Whistling Oyster — since 1907 — in a class by itself.

Whistling Oysters
Baked in Cream with Fresh Herbs

>   24 oysters, shucked, with their liquor
>   1 cup bread crumbs
>   2 cloves garlic, minced
>   small bunch parsley (leaves only)
>   ¼ cup clarified butter
>   8 Tbsp unsalted butter, softened
>   2 Tbsp fresh herbs, chopped — basil, tarragon, chervil, dill
>   salt and pepper
>   8 Tbsp heavy cream
>   chopped parsley for garnish
>   lemon wedges for garnish

Method — Mix bread crumbs, parsley, garlic, and clarified butter together. Divide half the crumb mixture evenly into four small ramekins which can be placed in the oven. Place six oysters and their liquor on the crumbs. Mix butter, herbs, and salt and pepper to taste. Divide the butter mixture evenly over the oysters. Top with remainder of the crumbs and top each ramekin with two tablespoons of heavy cream. Bake in preheated 375° oven for 15 minutes, or until bubbling. Top with chopped parsley and serve with lemon-wedge garnish.